Robert Leach

THE
FASHION RESOURCE BOOK
MEN

393 illustrations, 277 in color

CONTENTS

Foreword 6

Introduction 8

1 THE RESEARCH PROCESS

Research Practices 15

    Burberry 18

    Thom Browne 20

    Comme des Garçons 22

    Louis Vuitton: Kim Jones 24

    Sibling 26

    Yohji Yamamoto 28

    RRL by Ralph Lauren 30

    Nigel Cabourn 32

    Alexander McQueen 36

    The Vintage Showroom 38

    Christopher Shannon 40

2 RESEARCH AND INSPIRATION

Historical Research 43

    Archive and Museum 48

Trends and Forecasting 50

Street Style 52

    Garment Case Study: The Harrington Jacket 54

Style 56

    The Duke of Windsor 58

Popular Culture 62

Heritage 64

    Barbour 66

    C. P. Company/Aitor Throup 68

    Belstaff 70

To Tommy Nutter

(17 April 1943–17 August 1992)

Page 1 Basso & Brooke Stardust print.

Page 2 Basso & Brooke menswear.

The Fashion Resource Book: Men © 2014 Thames & Hudson Ltd, London

Text © 2014 Robert Leach

All Rights Reserved. No part of this publication may be reproduced or transmitted in any form or by any means, electronic or mechanical, including photocopy, recording or any other information storage and retrieval system, without prior permission in writing from the publisher.

First published in 2014 in paperback in the United States of America by Thames & Hudson Inc., 500 Fifth Avenue, New York, New York 10110

thamesandhudsonusa.com

Library of Congress Catalog Card Number 2013948278
ISBN 978-0-500-29132-0

Printed and bound in Malaysia by C.S. Graphics

World 72
    Case Study:
        Kelvin Kwok 76

Formal Wear 78
    Savile Row 80
    Case Study:
        Laurens Brunt 82
    Garment Case Study:
        Blazer Stripes 84
    Gieves & Hawkes 86
    Tommy Nutter 88
    Timothy Everest 90

Uniform 92
    Combat Kit 94
    Tropical Uniform 96
    Case Study:
        Aaron Tubb 98
    Stone Island 100
    Camouflage 104
    Ceremonial Uniform 108

Workwear 110
    Denim 114
    Levi Strauss 116
    Lee 118
    Carhartt WIP
        (Work in Progress) 120
    Contemporary Workwear 122
    Contemporary Denim 124

The Language of Clothes 126
    Garment Case Study:
        Oilskins 128
    Knit Case Study:
        Fair Isle 130

Sportswear 136
    Baseball and Letterman Jackets 138

Concept-Led and Avant-Garde 140
    Junya Watanabe 142
    Aitor Throup 144
    Case Study:
        Liam Hodges 146
    XXBC 148
    Case Study:
        Marios Alexandrou 150
    Case Study:
        James Pawson 152
    Bernhard Willhelm 154
    Walter Van Beirendonck 156

3 GARMENT BIOGRAPHIES

    The Trench Coat 160
    The Pea Coat 164
    Case Study:
        Philip Strawbridge 170
    The Parka 172
    The Motorcycle Jacket 178
    The Denim Jacket 182
    The Flying Jacket 188
    The Duffle Coat 194
    The Field Jacket 200

Bibliography 204
Acknowledgments 204
Illustration Credits 205
Index 206

FOREWORD

As course director for the BA Fashion Design at the University of Westminster, I'm often asked, 'What is it that makes a great fashion designer?' While it is true that great designers need to have an innate sense of colour, an eye for pleasing proportions and a grasp of spatial awareness to work in 3D around the body, what is more important than any of these is a hunger to innovate, which can only come through experimentation and research.

Good design does not come from rootless creative flights of fantasy with the designer sitting with sketchpad and pencil in hand. Designers need to be obsessive about research in all its forms, to know what has gone before and what is happening now, and then to be able to take a leap into the future and imagine what should be coming next.

Any successful design process, whether in a classroom or a professional design practice, always has research as its starting point. Good research makes connections that are both obvious and oblique; it tells us something new about ideas or styles we thought we knew all about.

Good designers, through the process of undertaking extensive and exhaustive research, are able to analyse, re-appropriate or sometimes even outright *steal* ideas from the past, and through the use of juxtaposition, caricature or exaggeration tell us something vital about our future.

In recent years there has been a growing focus and appreciation of menswear. While there is a commonality in approaches to the respective disciplines, what differentiates menswear from womenswear is the hidden subtext and codes of dress that to an untrained eye easily go unnoticed. Indeed, it is attention to these small but powerful subtleties and nuances that strengthens the success of a designer's work.

I have known Robert Leach for nearly twenty years as a practitioner, designer and educator, first at Central Saint Martins as a tutor, and now at the University of Westminster as a fellow educator. One of the key design projects that Robert teaches at Westminster is the second-year module 'Design for Sportswear'. Through in-depth research this project helps students to understand how to research and then make connections between historical and contemporary sportswear.

As a discipline, menswear has a long history of taking clothing that has a functional sportswear purpose and reinventing it to create the staple garments of menswear. Blazers, polo shirts and sweatshirts have all become indispensable in the modern man's wardrobe.

Designers, and in particular menswear designers, utilize real garments, be they vintage or modern, utilitarian or ceremonial, tailored or casual, as a legitimate source of design research. But they also recognize that it is how a garment is worn that makes it modern and gives it a sense of relevance to contemporary menswear.

Nineteenth-century Russian street vendor selling slippers.

However, far from merely recycling historical ideas, students are challenged to research the broader cultural context and think about issues surrounding menswear such as identity, sexuality, politics and power. The design projects at Westminster underpin the need for students to understand that creative innovation is in direct correlation to the depth of research that they undertake. The ability to take diverse and disparate visual research and arrange it in such a way as to make stimulating and thought-provoking connections is the key to creating a successful collection.

So where does this book fit in to all of this? *The Fashion Resource Book: Men* is a fantastic tool that shows how professional fashion designers use a variety of research methods to create menswear that is modern, contemporary and thrilling. The best menswear designers manage to honour the traditions and heritage of menswear while simultaneously creating innovation by pushing its codes forward.

As well as containing a wealth of visual imagery that clearly shows how practising designers construct their creative worlds, this book contains interviews with a variety of international menswear designers that enable us to understand how they, as individuals, approach their work and how personal research is key to their creativity.

These interviews give an unprecedented insight into a range of approaches to research in the design process. From Kim Jones and his take on upscale menswear luxe at Louis Vuitton, through Timothy Everest and his modern Savile Row style, to Nigel Cabourn with his vintage utilitarian aesthetic – all use extensive personal research as their starting point.

For both students and designers alike this book clearly shows the processes and practices that enable designers to create new approaches to research and produce menswear that is creative, exciting and innovative.

Andrew Groves
University of Westminster

INTRODUCTION

Men's fashion differs from womenswear in that it has a much tighter framework for the designer to work within. It is not about huge concepts and avant-garde silhouettes: as a discipline, menswear is much more rooted in reality – in product, if you like.

The roots of menswear can be easily traced over the centuries; the overcoats, the coats, the trousers and waistcoats of old all remain totally recognizable today. Men's fashion is often cyclical, just as womenswear can be: fads and fashions return.

Prior to the French Revolution (1789–99), the man had more often been the peacock, dressing in a brighter and more ostentatious way than his female counterpart. The revolution can be seen as a turning point whereby upper-class taste became more sombre, less conspicuously showy. While the dandies of the late eighteenth century are thought of as ostentatious, they actually led the way for simpler, less colourful fashions. Beau Brummell, renowned dandy and a friend of the Prince Regent, led this trend for more sombre, less embellished clothing. Frock coats were often black, dark green or dark blue, knee-length pantaloons became full length and, whereas they were once light-coloured – white or cream – they darkened to match the coat. The suit as we know it today had come into being, with the emphasis being much more on the cut.

Dark suits prevailed. By the time of the Industrial Revolution men in the Western world were almost always dressed in black suits with white starched shirts and stiff collars. Aristocracy and social standing in dress disappeared to some extent, although the initiated could easily discern the difference between rich and poor by the cut and fabric of their respective suits.

By the twentieth century, celebrities had come to influence fashion. In both England and the United States during the 1920s and 1930s, the Duke of Windsor (formerly King Edward VIII) had a huge impact on contemporary men's fashion. Then, as now, Hollywood film stars were also trendsetters.

In 1929 the Men's Dress Reform Party was founded by, among others, a psychologist at University College London named John Carl Flügel. For a decade it sought to lobby for the 'aesthetic liberation of men', perhaps as a backlash to the First World War and certainly as a result of the new interest in health and exercise. The movement, with its talk of eugenics, was linked with Nazism in the minds of some and eventually lost momentum. With or without this small group of reformists, change was certainly coming, although not immediately. Styles came and went, but the garments themselves essentially remained the same. The largest single change came with the concept of casualwear.

Before the Second World War, men, on the whole, wore either a suit or overalls to the workplace. Most men wore a cap or a hat, and weekend wear was a suit – 'Sunday best'. In the United States men in employment were

Nineteenth-century *cartes de visite* featuring, from left to right, upper-class, working-class and middle-class men.

defined by the colour of their collars: blue for manual labourers, as opposed to the starched white collar worn by desk workers.

In the first half of the 1940s, men around the world replaced their civilian clothing with the uniforms of various armed forces and ranks. Most clothes manufacturing was given over to the supply of uniforms, and a 'make do and mend' culture was born. In the United Kingdom the Utility scheme was set up by the government in 1941 to provide inexpensive quality clothing. The strict code promoted the use of smaller amounts of cloth with minimal trims and fastenings. The labels of these garments bore a CC41 logo, designed by Reginald Shipp, which stood for 'Civilian Clothing 1941' and signified that the clothing met wartime austerity regulations.

The British 'utility suit' and the American 'victory suit' were both made of new wool–synthetic blends, and had no pleats and turn-ups so as to minimize the amount of cloth used. Jackets were shorter in length and had no cuff buttons or patch pockets. Trousers were of a narrower cut and double-breasted suits were made without their usual waistcoats.

As the wartime rationing of fabrics came to an end, trousers became wider and turn-ups returned. In the United States *Esquire* championed the 'Bold Look' of wide shoulders and broad lapels. In the United Kingdom clothes rationing remained in place until 1949. Soldiers returning from war were provided with a 'demob' suit by the government ('demob' standing for 'demobilized'), usually in blue or grey chalk stripes. On handing over their uniform at one of the demobilization centres across the country they would be given a package containing either a three-piece suit or a single-breasted jacket and flannel trousers, a shirt with two detachable collars and studs, a pair of shoes and a felt hat or flat cap – my father married my mother in his demob suit. Many of these suits were manufactured by Montague Burton (of the high-street tailor Burton) at its factory in Leeds, England.

Dressing casually before the war might have consisted of removing one's jacket or rolling up one's shirt sleeves. Specific items of clothing catered to sports and leisure activities, including hunting jackets, golfing sweaters and riding breeches, but there was no truly generic casualwear. After the war, some of these garments began to be appropriated into casual attire. The T-shirt, previously an undergarment, began to be worn with blue jeans taken from workwear and teamed with a biker's jacket or a hunter's blouson jacket. The film stars and musicians of the day increasingly set the trends in the United States, and the styles made popular by them were quick to cross the Atlantic. The arrival of casual clothes and, for that matter, working-class fashion was a postwar phenomenon associated with rising wealth. The fashion theatre at the 1951 Festival of Britain, which heralded the release of the grip of wartime austerity, showcased the style of the 'new leisure wear'. In Britain, Burton made it possible for young men to purchase 'a five guinea suit for 55 shillings', while, in the United States, J. C. Penney and Sears sold to the young through their stores and mail-order businesses. For the first time, teenagers had disposable income, much of which they spent on the affordable fashions of the day.

London's Savile Row, the traditional home of bespoke tailoring, suffered severe damage in the Blitz, and struggled to recover, but by 1950 it was back in business. That was the year that *Harper's Bazaar* proclaimed the 'Return of the Beau' and Savile Row introduced the 'New Edwardian Look'. This featured a slightly flared jacket, natural shoulders and an overall narrower cut, worn with a curly-brimmed bowler hat and a long slender overcoat with velvet collar and cuffs. The style was copied by young working-class men, who became known as Teddy Boys. They accessorized with brightly coloured socks and bootlace ties, achieving what Richard Walker called a 'dizzy combination of Edwardian dandy and American gangster' (*The Savile Row Story*, Prion, 1988). The horrified establishment tailors of Savile Row dropped the Edwardian styling, but formal suits continued to move away from the broad English drape cut, and single-breasted two-piece suits with narrower lines and less padding in the shoulders became fashionable everywhere. Dark charcoal grey replaced the ubiquitous black, and the era of the grey flannel suit was born.

Later in the 1950s, a new Continental style of suit appeared

This caricature dating from 1796 shows fashionably dressed pedestrians on Bond Street, London. In the foreground, five men crowd a woman and girl off the path and into the muddy street, reversing standard etiquette in order to keep their own garments pristine.

Dressed in their entries for a competition organized by the Men's Dress Reform Party, five men stroll along Great Russell Street, London, near King George's Hall, scene of the event, 1937.

Overleaf, clockwise from top left
Demobilized soldiers and sailors leave Olympia, London, with their civilian clothes in boxes, 1945.

Breeches with the CC41 Utility mark, late 1940s.

In October 1936, protesters marched 480 km (300 miles) from Jarrow in northeast England to London to protest against high levels of unemployment.

from the fashion houses of Italy, with sharper shoulders, lighter fabrics (often with a sheen), shorter fitted jackets and narrower lapels.

In the United States, casual sport coats were being worn, generally following the lines of suit coats. Tartan plaids were fashionable in the early 1950s, and later plaids and checks of all types were worn, as were corduroy jackets with leather buttons. Khaki-coloured trousers, or chinos, were worn for casual occasions. Bermuda shorts, often in madras plaid, appeared mid-decade and were worn with knee socks. Knit shirts and sweaters of various kinds were popular throughout the period, while the rebellious look of jeans, leather jackets and white T-shirts popularized by Hollywood stars such as Marlon Brando in *The Wild One* (1953) and James Dean in *Giant* (1956) was taken up by teenagers and young men.

Fashion became the realm of the younger person, and subcultures proliferated, each with its own look. After the Teddy Boys of the 1950s came the mods and rockers of the 1960s, then the hippies and the psychedelic scene. The competing impulses of glam rock and skinheads dominated the first half of the 1970s, followed by the explosion of punk. Music and fashion subcultures have long been inextricably entwined: goths, indie kids, skater kids and hip-hop fans, among myriad others, all have their tribal niche, and elements of each subculture's style filter through to mainstream fashion.

Today's menswear tends to be trans-seasonal, with the male consumer expecting to wear a garment for more than six months. Quality and longevity therefore have to be built in, and men's fashion cannot be as trend-led as its female counterpart. Modern menswear is primarily about the detail, the fit and the cloth. It can be tribal – knowing, cliquey and exclusive. The male consumer is nothing if not a discerning one.

1
THE RESEARCH PROCESS

Research Practices 15
    Burberry 18
    Thom Browne 20
    Comme des Garçons 22
    Louis Vuitton: Kim Jones 24
    Sibling 26
    Yohji Yamamoto 28
    RRL by Ralph Lauren 30
    Nigel Cabourn 32
    Alexander McQueen 36
    The Vintage Showroom 38
    Christopher Shannon 40

RESEARCH PRACTICES

Menswear designers draw on many different sources for their research but always ground it in real clothing and function. No matter how mundane or indeed avant-garde the designer may appear to be, at the heart of his or her design work will be an authenticity of purpose, together with an awareness of menswear as a product as opposed to art (as sometimes happens in womenswear).

To be a successful menswear designer, a solid working knowledge of the history of menswear is vital, as is a familiarity with tailoring and with the history of uniform. Menswear is not about extreme silhouettes or superfluous detail; and it used to be less about colour and print than womenswear, although this has shifted over the past few years. The contemporary male consumer is a more discerning and probably braver one than his forebears.

Andrew Groves, course director at the University of Westminster, London, says: 'Womenswear designers as a whole, I think, are still stuck in a very old-fashioned way of designing, taking inspiration from abstract or ethereal subject matter, whereas menswear is far more about the technical, practical and functional nature of the designed garment. Even when menswear goes into fantasy, such as Thom Browne or Viktor & Rolf, it still has a functionality to it. So within the constraints of practicality, functionality and fantasy, they still balance.'

Ike Rust, senior menswear lecturer at London's Royal College of Art, comments: 'Currently menswear is about designers daring to be original and following through in their own way with ideas that are not generic or plagiarized. Fashion is hardly fashion any more; it's clothing dolled up through styling, which is the design quick-fix – and most people can't tell the difference.'

According to Stephanie Cooper, menswear lecturer at Central Saint Martins, London, 'Contemporary menswear design is driven by obsession to detail, reinvention and subversion of the traditional, and sensitive attention to fabrication, scale and proportion, where in some cases, the width of trouser or a lapel can become a life-changing event. Within this discipline, there are endless and inexhaustible possibilities to be explored.'

Sharon Graubard, senior vice president of trend analysis at Stylesight, New York, the world's leading online trend and prediction provider, agrees about the significance of detail. 'I think menswear has an advantage with having a smaller vernacular,' she says. 'That means that any tiny change – a higher neckline, a wider collar, a shorter leg, an unexpected colour – speaks volumes.'

Another very important component of good menswear design is fitness for function. For Groves, 'Menswear is really about pushing forward both from a technical and aesthetic viewpoint. Designers such as 6876,

MA.STRUM, Barbour, Henri Lloyd and Ten C are very much interested in evolving a product or functional garment. That is, the design is led by understanding the garment's use and functionality, how it needs to be adapted for modern use and contemporary society.

'These designers research from real garments – examples of workwear, military wear or utilitarian clothing. This thorough research would then be coupled with experimentation with the latest fabrics, or fabric treatments, to create something that is both authentic in its details yet modern in its manufacture and finish.'

Another key aspect of designing menswear is drawing on the history or heritage of the brand in question. The British outerwear label Barbour capitalizes on its rich heritage, while reinventing its product for the modern consumer much the same way that luxury brands Burberry and Louis Vuitton do. The success of the heritage phenomenon has led some brands to manufacture a sense of history that ignores their relatively recent origins. In the United Kingdom, Jack Wills and Hackett (founded in 1999 and 1979 respectively) trade successfully on their perceived longevity and sense of history. Similarly, Abercrombie & Fitch, although a long-running brand name (founded in 1892, but relaunched in the 1970s), is a relative newcomer, as is Ralph Lauren (operating since 1969); but again, both these companies are perceived to have a long and established legacy by customers eager to buy into the dream offered.

'Within the parameters that define menswear,' says Groves, 'there is so much scope for reinventing and reinterpreting the classic garments such as the two-piece suit, the trench coat, the Harrington jacket or the blazer. This ability to deconstruct and play with "classic" elements is what makes menswear so exciting.'

On the theme of more general research for menswear design, Sharon Graubard of Stylesight says that 'for designers everything is research; people at a party, kids on their way to school, film, art and so on. It's important to be artistically inspired but it's also important to understand a particular market, and for that, retailers, magazines and blogs are important touchpoints.'

It is important to research an area that appeals to you. As Ike Rust says: 'I encourage students to design based on what motivates them. If they have the boldness to work with what they love and are not afraid to honestly show who they are and what they are about, they are likely to contribute considerably to the discipline.

'I believe the source of a designer's inspiration is closely bound to their character. This is the one constant they have to offer and if they can identify and work with this it shapes them into true originals.

'The great dilemma comes when students are taught that research is an object rather than a process. They can collate up to a hundred pages of "research" images that they have no connection to and do not know how to work with.'

THE RESEARCH PROCESS 17

Above A mountaineering-inspired rucksack and blanket, Louis Vuitton Men, Autumn/Winter 2013. The collection was inspired by mountaineering and the Himalayan region of Bhutan.

Above right
Mountaineering-related mood boards by Aiden Weaver, University of Westminster, London.

Richard Gray is an illustrator and lecturer at Central Saint Martins, the University of Westminster and the Royal College of Art. 'With the more specific codes and vocabulary of men's clothing as opposed to women's,' he says, 'there are more opportunities to subvert, reinvent and find inspiration to create new ideas.'

As part of their research for menswear, Gray suggests that 'students go to the integral source of inspiration, given that so much menswear design can be inspired by core references: sportswear, military, tailoring, etc. That means going to vintage shops, army supplies, sportswear suppliers (both modern and vintage) or, for more obscure pieces, eBay, rather than looking at other designers' garments inspired by these references. I try to encourage my students to try to source real pieces so they can closely study the details of the components of these types of clothing. Their understanding of the reality of these garments is supplemented by images from books, visits to museums, etc. Hopefully, no matter how creative the students' reinterpretations or developments of these inspirations are through cut and construction, they are underpinned with an authenticity of deeper understanding and analysis.'

BURBERRY

Below **Burberry advertising from the 1920s featuring their iconic mac.**

Opposite left **Classic Burberry mac in a traditional colour.**

Opposite right **Burberry, Autumn/Winter 2012. Men's mac with college scarf detail to hem.**

THE RIDING BURBERRY
Very full skirts completely protect the knees and legs.
Burberry Gabardine recommended ; 10/6 more than price quoted for Walking pattern

Burberry was founded in Basingstoke, Hampshire, in 1856 by Thomas Burberry, a former draper's apprentice. By 1870, the business had begun to specialize in outerwear and set about developing its own hardwearing and weatherproof cloths, including gabardine. In 1901 the trademark logo of a knight on horseback together with the word 'Prorsum', Latin for 'forwards', was registered. The name Prorsum is now used for the ready-to-wear line. The Burberry brand became synonymous with practical and functional outerwear, and has had many associations with famous sportspeople, explorers and mountaineers.

Christopher Bailey joined Burberry in 2001 as creative director, and is, in part, credited with making the brand one of the biggest hitters in fashion today. Acutely aware of the brand's outerwear heritage, Bailey says that there are certain constants when designing for Burberry: 'Outerwear and all our different iconic coats, from duffles to pea coats to fisherman cabans to trench coats' (interview with Sally Bain, *westminsterfashion*, 2009).

Nowadays the headquarters are in London, and a 2,500 square metre (27,000 square foot) flagship store has opened on one of London's premier shopping streets, Regent Street.

For Bailey, the shop is a deliberate attempt to bring the online Burberry experience in-store. The shop features huge television screens, playing audio and visual content as well as live-streaming content. Radio-frequency-identification (RFID) chips are attached to certain items of clothing and accessories so that when a customer holding a garment approaches one of the screens, footage about that particular piece may be shown – whether that is of the item in a catwalk show, for example, or being manufactured.

Bailey said, in an interview in *The Guardian* in September 2012, 'People are interested in what goes behind products now. You can show so much more on the Web through video and text and moving imagery. So what we wanted to do, for example, is if I try on a trench coat and approach one of the mirrors that we've enabled with RFID, content comes up on the screen that shows how we've made that trench coat, what it looked like on the runway. We're putting stories behind clothes and fashion.'

In a separate interview for the University of Westminster magazine (Bailey was a student there), he said: 'Burberry is a company very much at the forefront of new technology, while keeping a firm grasp on its heritage and roots.'

THE RESEARCH PROCESS   19

THOM BROWNE

Describing his ideal customer as his muse, Thom Browne said, in a 2006 interview with Amy Larocca for *New York* magazine: 'He kind of does his thing and he has his life, and everything is very understated. His house is very lived in, but in a good way. It's not interior-decorated or anything like that, but it is decorated. He's health-conscious, but not too. He eats well, but he's not preoccupied: He will have cream and butter, and he will drink. And he's nice.'

Born in 1965 in Pennsylvania, Browne studied to be an economist before (after trying his hand at acting) going to work for the Ralph Lauren Corporation in New York, which he left in 2001 to start his own line. He began by designing just five suits, made by an Italian tailor in New York, which he wore around town himself. Inspired by his love of vintage tailoring, the suits have an almost cartoon look of the 1950s, with their Pee-wee Herman-esque cropped trousers and high-buttoning jackets with shrunken sleeves. In the last few years he has redefined tailoring: he has made the suit cool again.

Opposite Models wear brightly coloured creations in clashing madras, Thom Browne, Spring/Summer 2013, Paris.

Below Models wear Thom Browne suits outside Harrods, London, for the inaugural London Collections: Men, Spring/Summer 2013.

'I feel like jeans and a T-shirt have become Establishment,' said Browne. 'Everyone's dressed down. So actually putting on a jacket is the anti-Establishment stance.'

Browne has collaborated with the classic American brand Brooks Brothers on its Black Fleece range and works for the French company Moncler, where he has been designing the Gamme Bleu range since 2009.

In addition to the suit range and his work elsewhere, Browne also shows seasonally in Paris with love-it-or-hate-it collections, which in their avant-garde styling and usually riotous patterns and colours are the total antithesis of his trademark grey suits. But, as Tim Blanks pointed out on Style.com, 'they're all in the service of that grey flannel suit – the shows are gaudy bejeweled fantasias that highlight the humble gold ring in their midst.'

COMME DES GARÇONS

Rei Kawakubo, born in Tokyo in 1942, is notoriously silent or oblique about her influences. Sometimes she might utter one word – possibly an abstract concept – about a particular collection. Her inspirations are often difficult to pin down and indefinable, but on closer inspection Comme des Garçons menswear is always rooted in real, and often historical, clothing. Kawakubo started her Comme des Garçons menswear range in 1978, and it has been designed by Junya Watanabe since then. The Homme Plus menswear range was started in 1984, followed by the Comme des Garçons shirt range in 1988 – a range of shirts manufactured in France and at a lower price point than the main line.

Despite her associations with modernism, and its eschewing of nostalgia, nineteenth-century tailoring influences are sometimes very apparent in Kawakubo's collections, and the garments display clear and evident research into the period. Also seen are the definite influences of workwear of all kinds and other specific garment types: the biker jacket, for example, reappears frequently in her collections, as do the duffel coat, the frock coat and many other classic garments. These are often subverted, either by fabric choice (she is particularly known for her experimentation with fabric development for tactile pleasure) or by an exaggeration of cut. Garments might have outlandish styling or be shown with unexpected pairings or proportions. Sometimes, unusual historical or cultural references are used, such as the folding and draping associated with traditional Japanese clothing or the workwear of Japanese fishermen fused with traditional Western tailoring.

The Autumn/Winter 2012 collection shown here was named 'Neither Man Nor Woman' and was described by Tim Blanks on Style.com as being 'in the shadow land between the New York Dolls and the girls of St Trinian's'. With its sexless and slightly androgynous aesthetic, the collection featured brocade frock coats, hats with moiré ribbons and bows to the neck – things more usually associated with womenswear. Throw large tricorne hats worn with cape coats into the mix and we ended up with a collection that would not have looked too unfamiliar to a gentleman of the eighteenth century.

Above and opposite **Comme des Garçons menswear, Autumn/Winter 2012, Paris.**

LOUIS VUITTON: KIM JONES

For natural-history buff Kim Jones, menswear designer at Louis Vuitton, travel is vitally important to him as a designer: it feeds his inspiration.

'What inspires me most is travel; where you can visit the places, see and experience them, and see the real story,' he says. 'I travel everywhere I can, and as much as possible, to get inspired. My work at Vuitton always embodies an element of travel, as that is what the house is built on. I look at places and moments in time that can be drawn on to create something new.'

To research the Autumn/Winter 2013 collection, Jones travelled to the Kingdom of Bhutan in the Himalayas. He explains: 'I was looking for somewhere close to the Karakoram region, where the famous Louis Vuitton blankets are made, and Bhutan, with its exotic culture and wildlife, struck me as a perfect research destination.'

The collection featured a technically fascinating snow leopard textile, fabricated by needle-punching an underlay of mink through a luxury cashmere fabric, and a custom print designed by British artists Jake and Dinos Chapman. Named 'Garden in Hell', it depicted lush foliage and mythical Himalayan creatures, evoking the rich heritage and mystery of this part of the world. Elsewhere, yak felt and reindeer skins were used, hard grey stones from the Himalayas were fashioned into cufflinks, and traditional Bhutanese checks and stripes were woven into British suitings. In keeping with the Himalayan research, coats were belted with mountaineer's ropes tipped with silver and there were Stephen Jones-designed Sherpa hats.

Describing his research methods, Jones talks about how they 'tend to always come from my personal style and I then apply it to the lifestyle of the Louis Vuitton man; someone that is very much at home anywhere in the world.

'When I was designing for my own line it was very much about youth culture, and when I was at Dunhill it was about the history of the brand when it was great. With Vuitton it's about taking a legacy and moving it forward – the brand is very directional even though it is steeped in tradition. All in all it's about the needs of the modern man; I guess I'm one of them so I always have elements that reflect me.

'I'm an obsessive researcher and spend most of my time researching many things. I like to get to the purest form of something to then move forward again. It's something that has led me to be quite a collector of books, clothing and art, as well as many other things.'

Something that has made a difference, says Jones, is that 'these days I have more finance, which enables me to find some of the rarer pieces and perhaps reference books that other people can't. It allows me to travel widely to find inspiration, which is really the key part.'

> 'A picture might be worth a thousand words, but actually being in a place is worth a million.'
> Kim Jones

Himalayan-inspired collection, Louis Vuitton Men, Autumn/Winter 2013, Paris.

SIBLING

London-based knitwear company Sibling was formed by Joe Bates, Sid Bryan and Cozette McCreery in 2008. Their intention, they said, was to 'give men's knitwear a good old-fashioned shake-up with cartoon-style ka-pows of colour and bams of very English humour'.

To this end, for their first collection they played with subverting classic knitwear, bringing new and unexpected techniques to the jaded genre of men's knits. We saw sequinned leopard-spot twinsets and sparkling Breton sweaters.

For their second collection they played further with subversion, which was fast becoming their trademark. What seemed at first glance to be a traditional leather biker jacket, on closer inspection revealed itself to be fully knitted in a black cotton yarn and then laminated to mimic worn leather; and what appeared to be a classic denim jacket was also totally knitted, this time with indigo-dyed yarn.

The trio's Autumn/Winter 2011 collection, titled 'Darn the Boozer', took inspiration from the designers' favourite pubs in the East End of London. The Golden Heart pub gave rise to a crew-neck sweater with an embroidered tattoo-style heart and spider's-web elbows; the Bricklayer's Arms resulted in a zipped, varsity-style knitted jacket with an embroidered coat of arms on the back. To evoke The Red Lion pub, the trio produced a sweater featuring

Below and opposite bottom
Sibling's Fair Isle-inspired sweaters with motifs by artist Will Broome, 2010.

Above Sibling's punk-inspired slogan knitwear, Spring/Summer 2011.

Above right Sibling's 'Panda Rocks' sweater and balaclava, 2011.

the eponymous feline. For the George & Dragon, they designed a traditional Fair Isle sweater, knitted in Scotland, but instead of the usual geometric stitches it featured such motifs as crossed cigarettes, dragons and, naturally, St George himself.

The three have gone on to explore their pop aesthetic with various collaborations and cite as influences everything from the British funfair and fast food to the outrageous transsexual punk musician Wayne/Jayne County. It is this mix of the mundane with the extraordinary that keeps their work so fresh and exciting.

YOHJI YAMAMOTO

'When I started a men's line in Paris, my message was very simple: let's be outside of this. Let's be far from our suits and ties. Let's be far from businessmen. Let's be vagabonds.'

Yohji Yamamoto was born in Tokyo in 1943. He first came to the attention of the Western fashion press in 1981 after showing in Paris at the invitation of the Chambre Syndicale de la Couture Parisienne. His all black collections at the time led the designer to explain that a lack of colour 'focuses the eye on the cut' and conveys a sense of being 'modest and arrogant at the same time'.

During the 1980s, his signature baggy black suit jacket and wide trousers, worn with a white T-shirt, became the uniform for the well-dressed man in the creative or artistic fields – the advertising executive, the architect, the film director.

In an 1983 interview with John Duka in *The New York Times*, Yamamoto said, in his typically enigmatic way, 'I always wonder who decided that there should be a difference in the clothes of men and women. Perhaps men decided this.'

In 1989 German film director Wim Wenders made a documentary about this often mysterious and secretive designer. In the film, called *Notebook on Cities and Clothes*, the designer describes how he seeks inspiration not only from Japanese men's workwear but also from the early twentieth-century photographic portraits by German photographer August Sander.

Begun in 1911, Sander's most famous work, *People of the Twentieth Century*, is a series of portraits of archetypes divided into seven sections: The Farmer, The Skilled Tradesman, The Woman, Classes and Professions, The Artist, The City and The Last People (the homeless and disenfranchised).

This body of work by Sander is cited by both Yamamoto and Rei Kawakubo of Comme des Garçons as a major influence on their menswear designs. The influence of Sander's work is clearly discernible in Yamamoto's advertising and again in the eclectic casting of models for his catwalk presentations, where the young walk with the old and unconventional looking; the farmer with the artist.

Opposite Yohji Yamamoto, Autumn/Winter 2008. The coat and hat are reminiscent of clothing worn by early twentieth-century railway and telegraph workers.

This page Young men working as postal telegraph messengers in the United States, 1910s.

RRL
BY RALPH LAUREN

Founded in 1993, the RRL brand was created, according to its website, 'as a tribute to the independent spirit of the untamed West and the tireless resolve of the American worker'. The brand name and logo derive from Ralph Lauren's RRL cattle ranch in Colorado, which is held up as 'exemplify[ing] the soul and lifestyle of the brand'.

The design ethos of Double RL is to replicate and reproduce the finest classic menswear garments using the very best traditional materials and manufacturing techniques – those perennial favourites such as American-made hand-finished selvedge jeans, for example. These are made from denim woven in Japan on traditional 28- to 32-inch looms, then assembled in the United States with American-made threads, rivets and leather patches; the brand boasts that no two pairs are ever exactly alike.

British tweeds are woven in Leeds, England, at the area's only remaining 'vertical' mill, dating back to 1937. There RRL's herringbone, twills and plain tweeds are spun, dyed and woven.

The company cites the distinctive knitting of the Cowichan people of Canada's Pacific Northwest as another big inspiration. Cowichan designs, including both geometric and figurative motifs, were – and still are – passed down the generations. These designs are adapted for RRL's heavy hand-knitted sweaters. Also inspiring its knits are other traditional techniques, such as the Irish Aran, with its cable forms said to derive from a traditional Celtic pattern and the knots and nets of the fishermen who first wore them to the Scottish Fair Isle technique, from which RRL re-creates vintage patterns in the finest yarns.

American deerskin from a tannery in the Adirondack Mountains is used for leather jackets and shoes. Other staples include authentic-looking reproductions of the finest cotton chinos and other 'army surplus' items such as cotton twill GI shirts and bomber jackets.

What binds all this together is the integrity of materials and manufacture; there is an inherent quality, style and timelessness to all the brand's products.

Opposite and above **Interior shots of RRL stores.**

Right **RRL, Autumn/Winter 2003.**

NIGEL CABOURN

Nigel Cabourn has worked in the fashion industry for more than forty years, but his clothing has little in common with most people's concept of the word 'fashion'. He is influenced not by trends but a long-standing passion for vintage clothing, fabrics and details. These elements have formed the basis for much of his output over the years and continue to be a vital part of his collection today.

Cabourn has collected vintage clothing for more than three decades and has an archive of more than four thousand pieces, including salvaged British Military uniforms and workwear and a trove of exploration garments unearthed from all corners of the globe. It is this ever-increasing archive that is the cornerstone of his collections, rather than a particular trend or general demand. Each collection has a real story, a sense of history and integrity underpinned by the highest level of quality.

'Generally when working on a new collection,' says Cabourn, 'I am inspired by the historical event first. Then from that event I take a lot of interest in the specific clothing that was worn during that period. Therefore, both the historical reference and the clothing are important for the eventual research. For example, it was recently the hundredth anniversary of when Scott reached the Pole, and that then became the main feature of the collection.'

The original inspiration for the Authentic line was Edmund Hillary and the 1953 ascent of Everest; it was launched in 2003 to coincide with the fiftieth anniversary. The clothes worn during this remarkable human

Below and opposite
Nigel Cabourn photographs and garment details.

THE RESEARCH PROCESS 33

Vintage Military

achievement were basically all military in origin but had been customized for the climb. Cabourn owned many of the originals in his collection so he set about re-creating them as faithfully as possible. He used British manufacturers and original British fabrics to produce a collection without compromise; when a component was no longer available, Cabourn had it specially made.

Cabourn says: 'My archive is always growing and has been for the last thirty-five years. I would say in the last five years I have bought new vintage pieces at least six to ten times a year. In fact, on all my visits abroad it usually includes a trip to some unique vintage store.'

Nigel Cabourn has a great appreciation and knowledge of Japanese fabrics and has used them in his collections for many years. His Mainline collection gives him the chance to produce a specialist collection based on Japanese fabrics and production techniques that are not available in the United Kingdom.

The two collections – Authentic and Mainline – start with the same concept, but with Mainline being made in Japan it evolves differently by using various unique contemporary Japanese fabrics, finishes and washing techniques. Cabourn travels to Japan four times a year to work on design and fabrication to personally approve each prototype. He also works with some of the best Japanese mills to develop new fabrics based on original vintage fabrics from his archival collection. He pays particular attention to Japanese accessories to give Mainline the same integrity and attention to detail as Authentic.

Which is his favourite piece in the archive is, for Cabourn, 'a very tough question to answer as I have so many pieces. To be honest every trip I take I buy a vintage piece and this becomes my favourite!

'If I had to decide on just one piece though, it would be the cold weather parka which was worn by the British forces in World War II and also worn by some of the explorers going across the Antarctic.'

Right and opposite
Nigel Cabourn labels and advertisement.

THE VINTAGE SHOWROOM

The Vintage Showroom was founded by Douglas Gunn and Roy Luckett in 2007 to house their substantial archive of vintage clothing and accessories. The pair are passionate and knowledgeable about vintage menswear and The Vintage Showroom has grown to become one of the leading resources in the United Kingdom.

The archive covers mostly the early to mid-twentieth century and specializes in workwear and military and sports clothing from around the globe, as well as classic British tailoring and country wear.

The showroom is packed full of wonderful pieces of American denim and workwear, as well as early pieces by iconic brands, such as Belstaff, stacks of beautiful hand-knitted Fair Isle sweaters and lovely striped boating and cricket blazers from the 1920s.

For anyone interested in menswear it is an absolute treasure trove of inspiration. It is easy to understand why menswear designers are falling over themselves to visit; there is really no substitute for actually handling vintage pieces. Feeling the weight of the fabric, seeing how things are cut and constructed, and getting a real sense of the piece simply cannot be gained from the Internet or a book illustration.

The Vintage Showroom's business and collection is divided into two parts – a private showroom in west London and a retail outlet located in Covent Garden. The showroom's enormous collection of specially sourced and selected vintage clothing is available to view on an appointment-only basis; top brands and design studios, press and stylists from film and advertising all use this massively valuable resource.

Below **Vintage denim on display at The Vintage Showroom warehouse.**

Below right **European cagoule covered in souvenir patches.**

Opposite **American gilet with souvenir patches and badges.**

THE RESEARCH PROCESS 37

ALEXANDER MCQUEEN

Lee Alexander McQueen was born in London in 1969. He left school at sixteen and went to work as an apprentice in London's Savile Row, the home of bespoke tailoring, before going on to work for the theatre costumiers Angels, Berman's and Nathan's. Both types of training can be seen to have had a profound influence on his later work, with its propensity towards sharp tailoring and historical references.

McQueen graduated from the Central Saint Martins MA course in 1994 and set up his own label in London's East End. After building a successful womenswear business, famed for its extravagant and theatrical presentations, McQueen launched his first menswear collection in the spring of 2005, which led Tim Blanks to comment on Style.com: '...but the dramatics couldn't overshadow the true power of McQueen's tailored pieces. What he's mastered with his menswear is an easy, instinctive sensuality that is often missing from his women's collections.'

In the same year McQueen began a collaboration with sports company Puma to create a range of trainers, and in 2006 the McQ line launched, intended as a younger, less expensive diffusion line for both sexes.

McQueen died in February 2010, and the company is headed up by his former design assistant Sarah Burton, also a Central Saint Martins graduate. Burton continues to draw on the brand's rich design and research legacy. Collections include film and literary references, as well as allusions to the artists and photographers that inspired the great designer during his lifetime.

Above *Self Portrait in the Studio* by Claude-Emile Schuffenecker. The artist wears paint-streaked clothing similar to McQueen's designs for his Spring/Summer 2010 collection.

Opposite *Trompe l'œil* art-inspired pieces, Alexander McQueen, Spring/Summer 2010.

Pictured opposite are two outfits from the last menswear collection that McQueen designed, for Spring/Summer 2010, which was described in the company's press release thus: 'The creative process is often psychologically complex, and this season Alexander McQueen takes a look into the mind, and the wardrobe, of an artist.'

A short film by David Sims accompanied the static presentation of the collection. The clothes appeared to be smeared with paint and chalk; knitwear came with holes; the jackets sported hand-painted 'braiding'; and the crumpled trousers bore handprints. With a further nod to the artist as muse, the models wore Joseph Beuys-style fedora hats.

Everest Parka
Wide Lapel Harris Tweed Jacket
Harris Tweed Vest
Silk Bow Tie

CHRISTOPHER SHANNON

Liverpool-born Christopher Shannon graduated from the MA course at Central Saint Martins in 2008, and in 2010 received sponsorship from NEWGEN MEN for the Autumn/Winter season.

Shannon says that when researching for a collection he does not really have any particular starting points. In fact, 'there's no real stop point,' he says. 'We work all year in the studio and there is no massive break between collections. So some things overlap or have been put to one side from the season before. I am very into photography books, so I'm always going to my favourite bookshops or seeing book dealers – constantly building a library of imagery that I'm interested in. This goes from travel photography to skate books to very British archive imagery. I don't really look to fashion for ideas, although we do look for new shapes all the time: anything that can inform the finish of the pieces. Then there will be something else that I'm into at the time; more often than not it's something like a documentary or an album I've been really into, transferring that feeling or finding out what it is I like about it. Also constantly researching fabrics, which is one of the hardest things.'

As a designer Shannon feels it is important to look to the past for reference, yet without slavishly copying that past. 'All research exists in the past, so it's essential really,' he says. 'I'm not one for historical references; I'm more interested in passing moments and imagery than definite periods in time. With most people doing Internet research the time scope is pretty limited. I think it's really important to look in places other people aren't. I love finding older pieces that have a quality to them that you don't find so much now, and that can be really crude older sportswear or older designer pieces. With so many clothes being made in China and in such massive numbers I think it's easy to lose the appreciation for things that are a bit more considered. I think it's important to look to the past in general though, across all the disciplines, to understand the order and dialogue of things.'

Shannon's Autumn/Winter 2013 collection was named 'Obsessive Compulsive Re-order'. His inspiration for the collection came as a result of 'watching loads of documentaries about people who are compulsive hoarders'. The ensuing eclectic mix of cable-knit sweaters, leather shirts and gaffer-taped jeans Shannon called 'anti-outfits'. The models sported greasy hair that looked as if it had not been washed for a few days – inspired by, Shannon explains, 'a boy I went to school with whose nickname was Spaghetti Head, as he had this really incredibly straight long hair. He could decide if he wanted to be a goth or a scally, he hovered in between – and I liked that indecision.'

Below **Christopher Shannon's ruffled shirts for Autumn/Winter 2011.**

Opposite **Christopher Shannon's design and development sheets for his Autumn/Winter 2011 collection.**

THE RESEARCH PROCESS 41

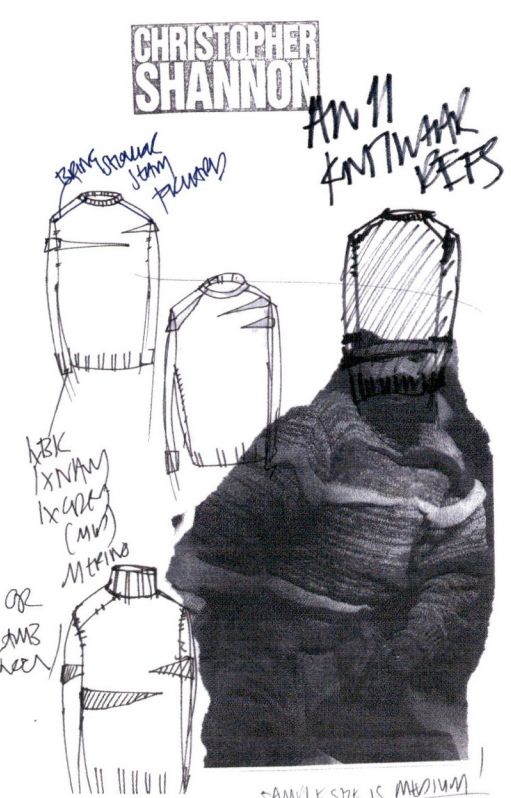

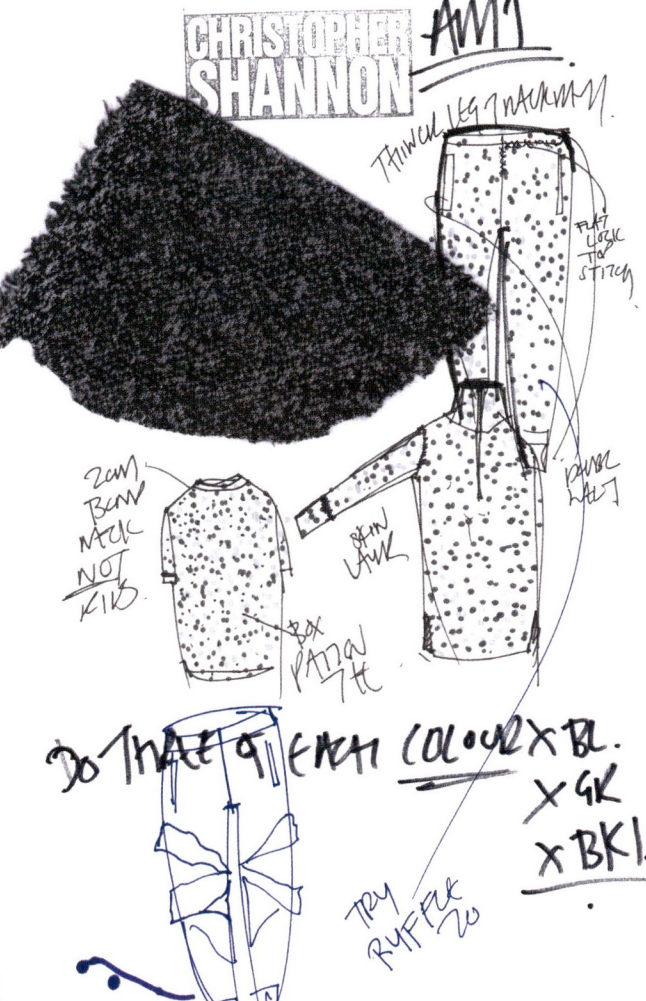

2
RESEARCH AND INSPIRATION

Historical Research 43
   Archive and Museum 48
Trends and Forecasting 50
Street Style 52
   Garment Case Study:
   The Harrington Jacket 54
Style 56
   The Duke of Windsor 58
Popular Culture 62
Heritage 64
   Barbour 66
   C. P. Company/
   Aitor Throup 68
   Belstaff 70
World 72
   Case Study:
   Kelvin Kwok 76
Formal Wear 78
   Savile Row 80
   Case Study:
   Laurens Brunt 82

Garment Case Study:
Blazer Stripes 84
   Gieves & Hawkes 86
   Tommy Nutter 88
   Timothy Everest 90
Uniform 92
   Combat Kit 94
   Tropical Uniform 96
   Case Study:
   Aaron Tubb 98
   Stone Island 100
   Camouflage 104
   Ceremonial Uniform 108
Workwear 110
   Denim 114
   Levi Strauss 116
   Lee 118
   Carhartt WIP
   (Work In Progress) 120
   Contemporary Workwear 122
   Contemporary Denim 124

The Language of Clothes 126
   Garment Case Study:
   Oilskins 128
   Knit Case Study:
   Fair Isle 130
Sportswear 136
   Baseball and
   Letterman Jackets 138
Concept-Led and Avant-Garde 140
   Junya Watanabe 142
   Aitor Throup 144
   Case Study:
   Liam Hodges 146
   XXBC 148
   Case Study:
   Marios Alexandrou 150
   Case Study:
   James Pawson 152
   Bernhard Willhelm 154
   Walter Van Beirendonck 156

HISTORICAL RESEARCH

Many designers look to the past for inspiration. In fact, menswear as a genre, based as it is on traditional cuts, functions and shapes, could be said to have changed little over time – futuristic visions in menswear rarely seem to cut it. Forward-thinking elements are usually limited to fabric technology and manufacturing processes, rather than any ground-breaking innovations in silhouette and design. The modern impulse manifests itself in a more minimalist approach to cut and colour that evokes a sense of architectural simplicity, such as we see, for example, in the menswear of Calvin Klein, Jil Sander, Raf Simons or Richard Nicoll.

The more thematic designers, such as Vivienne Westwood, Marc Jacobs, Alexander McQueen and John Galliano, often associate a collection with a specific place and time. Even the more cerebral designers do not shy away from this design method from time to time: Comme des Garçons, Junya Watanabe and even Prada have presented collections of menswear that were very much rooted in the past.

For her Spring/Summer 2012 collection, Miuccia Prada delivered a distinctly 1950s-flavoured collection with rockabilly-style pegged trousers, blouson jackets and short-sleeved shirts with 1950s-inspired prints, which were to become the menswear must-have of the season and would go on to inspire a thousand cheaper copies.

When Galliano was at the helm of his eponymous menswear brand, collections were almost always a fantastical mash-up of historical, artistic and geographical research. His well-received collection of Autumn/Winter 2008 is a good example: it took as inspiration the frost fairs that used to take place on the River Thames during winter months, when the river froze over completely and the whole of Tudor London came out to party, with aristocrats mixing with costermongers and vagrants.

Vivienne Westwood often harks back to historical menswear for her inspiration. Her first ever menswear collection, the highly influential 'Cut and Slash', shown in Florence in 1990, was based on the Tudor fashion of cutting and slashing clothing. This fashion was brought about by sumptuary laws, which dictated the colours and types of garments – including furs, fabrics and trimmings – that were allowed to be worn by people of given social ranks and occupations. Such laws were intended to reduce the nation's expenditure on imported textiles, as well as to reinforce class distinctions. They proved difficult to enforce, however, and men and women took to slashing the outer fabrics of their doublets or gowns to reveal the brighter lining fabrics beneath, thereby enlivening the drab colours of their outer clothes and making them appear more decorative.

In 2009 Joseph Corre (the son of Vivienne Westwood and Malcolm McLaren) and Simon 'Barnzley' Armitage set up their menswear label, A Child of the Jago, named after Arthur Morrison's Victorian novel of that

name. The novel is set in a fictional slum in East London called Jago, which was based on a real area called Old Nichol, where Corre and Armitage's shop is now located. Their label was set up, they say, 'in the face of manufacturing mediocrity and the attrition of craftsmanship since Britain's bygone days as an industrial power.... Cheap tricks of the new profiteer; "built-in-obsolescence", "value-engineering", "rapid promotional rotation" and "celebrity product-seeding" all conspire in an attempt to make monkeys out of us. For Fall 2010, A Child of the Jago shows us what can happen when the monkeys realize who has the real control.' The clothes were inspired by their favourite pieces and periods: military jackets, Edwardian Teddy Boy drape jackets and 1930s-gangster styling mixed with ethnic prints. Their collections have all the eclecticism of those early Westwood/McLaren collections such as 'Witches' and 'Buffalo'.

At Alexander McQueen, menswear has always been rooted in the late Lee Alexander McQueen's personal passions – those of traditional Savile Row menswear, formal military tailoring and his own brand of darkness inspired by Victorian gothicism of the past and the moodily envisioned future of the film *Blade Runner* (1982).

The Japanese designers Rei Kawakubo and Yohji Yamamoto often speak of their obsession with nineteenth- and early twentieth-century menswear of all ranks of society. Workwear and formal wear inspire their designs for men as well as women, particularly as depicted in the beautiful portraits by the early twentieth-century German photographer August Sander.

Portraiture, both painted and photographic, is an excellent source of reference for historical research, and invariably a much more worthy source of reference than any illustrated history-of-costume sourcebook.

'History is always key for menswear, because the silhouettes haven't really changed all that much in over a hundred years,' says Sharon Graubard of Stylesight, New York. 'So everything is available: Edwardian jackets, little rounded club collars, forties gangsters, fifties *Mad Men* suits, sixties hippies, seventies hipsters, eighties punk, nineties grunge – it's all part of the menswear vernacular. And then there is workwear, military uniforms, Western wear, sports clothing – and all of it is perfectly understandable for everyday menswear.'

Socialite Richard Colley is seen immaculately dressed in twinset and flannels with four salukis, 1920s.

RESEARCH AND INSPIRATION 47

Opposite **DAKS** advertisement, 1950s.

Clockwise from top **Three 1950s Hawaiian printed shirts.**

Left **1950s research materials by Rebecca Neilson, University of Westminster, London.**

ARCHIVE AND MUSEUM

While books and the Internet are good research facilities, there is nothing better than seeing things close up, studying them in three dimensions and getting a sense of scale, of material and of how things are manufactured and put together. To this end, museums and archives remain the best possible place to study historical garments.

Most cities have a museum, and capital cities in particular usually carry large costume collections. There are notable collections and specialist museums worldwide; the Victoria and Albert Museum in London has a splendid variety of costumes, and the Fashion and Textiles Museum in Bermondsey, south London, regularly mounts themed fashion exhibitions. Bath Museum of Costume is notable, as is the Museum of London. For studying all types of uniform the Imperial War Museum in south London is unbeatable. In Antwerp, Belgium, the fashion museum MoMu (Mode Museum) is renowned for its exhibitions, as are, in the United States, the Metropolitan Museum of Art in New York and the Philadelphia Museum of Art. Washington, DC, has a splendid Textile Museum, and the Los Angeles County Museum of Art, the Museum at FIT (Fashion Institute of Technology) in New York, and the Chicago History Museum are well worth a visit, either in person or via the Internet.

These are just a few examples and there are many smaller specialist museums and collections that are equally noteworthy.

Designer Paul Smith in an interview said: 'As such, anything can inspire, but in terms of actual research most museums will allow you to look at their archives or give you specific information if you plan it well in advance and make an appointment. People don't realize the opportunity there is to talk to curators or researchers and to delve into the archives.' Similarly, fashion lecturer Richard Gray advises designers to visit 'any museum or place that gives you access to the original source, not just printed visual depictions of it; the Victoria and Albert Museum, the Wellcome Collection, flea markets and vintage shops are all major sources of inspiration'.

Many brands and designers have built up their own archives. Nigel Cabourn has an extensive collection of more than four thousand pieces, and Stone Island in Italy has warehouses full of not only its own garments but also 'found' garments – often utilitarian pieces on which it bases its designs. In addition to such private archives, commercial archives exist that designers are able to visit for research and inspiration (see p. 38).

Left **Bootjack with First World War army officer's field boots, binoculars and camera case.**

Below **Bernhard Willhelm, Spring/Summer 2009.** Ensemble inspired by late sixteenth-century fashions similar to those shown in this portrait by Salomon Mesdach. Displayed at the 'Masters of Black in Fashion & Costume' exhibition at MoMu, Antwerp.

TRENDS AND FORECASTING

The notion that trends come solely from the catwalk has been somewhat turned on its head – a trend these days is every bit as likely to come from the street as from an international designer. A queue of people waiting outside a venue for a fashion show will probably receive just as much press attention as the clothes on the catwalk inside. Nowadays, magazines and the Internet are full of trend-spotters, and journalists and photographers travel between cities searching for emerging trends and inspirational people. Fashion forecasting has become big business.

Designers themselves often look to the street for inspiration. Trends emerge around the world that can fuel their imaginations. Among the first designers who really looked to street style in this context was Jean Paul Gaultier during the 1980s, who cited London's varied youth cultures as inspiration on various occasions.

Many designers and brands rely on fashion-forecasting businesses to deliver style, trend and colour prediction. Often they simply do not have the resources or the staff to be out and about all the time scrutinizing the trend and style information and presenting it in a clear and defined manner, so they hire professionals to do that job for them.

Among the bit hitters in this trend and forecasting industry is Stylesight, based in New York, London, Hong Kong and Shanghai, with offices and representatives all over the world. The company, formed in 2003, caters to style professionals involved in the creative design and product development processes who can use Stylesight's 'creative platform' to make the design journey faster, more efficient and more accurate.

At the same time, the catwalks retain a huge influence. Senior vice president of trend analysis Sharon Graubard of Stylesight comments: 'The runways are invaluable. Watching key, innovative designers and analysing what they choose to show each season, and how they put it all together, is very inspiring. Often it is the collection that at first appears repellent that offers the most inspiration. It is worthwhile contemplating the collections and "cracking the code" each season.'

These pages **Straight-up 'stylesightings' courtesy of Stylesight.**

STREET STYLE

Street style – the everyday clothes worn by people on the streets – has become both a fascination and an inspiration for designers and journalists alike. Many of today's fashion trends are said to start on the street. In the late 1970s photographer Bill Cunningham recorded the ordinary and not-so-ordinary people on the streets of New York, first for *Women's Wear Daily*, and later for *The New York Times*. He continues to do so to this day, as well as producing a weekly online slideshow for *The New York Times*, aptly named 'On The Street'. Talking about his work, Cunningham said in *The New York Times*: 'It isn't what I think; it's what I see. I let the street speak to me. You've got to stay on the street and let the street tell you what it is.'

In the United Kingdom, Terry Jones's *i-D* magazine, first published in 1980, pioneered the 'straight-up' style of photography, commissioning London's young photographers to document the city's street styles and its many varied subcultures. New Romantics rubbed shoulders with goths and skinheads, fashion and art students with young journalists, graphic designers with other creatives. The featured people gave details of what they were wearing and where it was from, a format that served essentially as the blueprint for so many of today's fashion blogs.

One of the most widely read fashion-related blogs on the Internet today is Swiss-born Yvan Rodic's 'Face Hunter', which he started in 2006. Rodic comes from a background in advertising and his style has been called 'a fresh DIY approach to fashion photography': the site comprises his own particular take on street-style photography, featuring portraits of individuals whose style grabs his attention. 'Face Hunter' was at the forefront of what has become an Internet phenomenon – style blogging.

Street style no longer consists of only the various subcultures and tribes, although they definitely still exist. Today it is every bit as much about individuality, self-expression and innovation in dress.

New York blogger, designer and street photographer Alex Lee, whose work is featured here, comments: 'I hope my work can be a daily source of interest and inspiration, helping some to change their perspectives of style and to embrace the subjectivity of it all.'

On the subject of men's street style, Sharon Graubard of Stylesight says: 'I love the men in New York, who lately have been sporting plenty of facial hair downtown and in Brooklyn; but uptown dandyism continues to gain momentum, with men playing with whimsical tailored clothing and bow ties. I was in Paris last week, and the weather was warm, and I was thrilled to see young men wearing tailored short suits, in a natural and easy way. Amsterdam always makes me happy for menswear, because the men look masculine and uncontrived, but still somehow look fashionable. It's about a consciousness – I call it "dressing with intent".'

Opposite
Top row **New York street-style shots by Alex Lee.**

Middle row **Street-style shot on left by Alex Lee**; others courtesy of Stylesight.

Bottom row **Street-style shot on left by Alex Lee**; others courtesy of Stylesight.

GARMENT CASE STUDY
THE HARRINGTON JACKET

Opposite Actor Steve McQueen wearing a Harrington jacket, with his wife Nellie, January 1963.

Right A skinhead in a Harrington jacket c. 1980.

Dating back to the 1960s, skinhead culture was an offshoot of the mod movement. More likely to be working class and less dandified than their 'smooth' mod counterparts, skinheads were initially a non-political subculture that grew from a love of early West Indian reggae, rocksteady and ska music. There are now many different types of skinhead but the original look was defined by their cropped hair, Fred Perry shirts and trousers worn cropped or rolled up to show off their Dr Martens boots. The Harrington jacket was often an integral part of the look.

Right and below
Baracuta G9 Harrington jacket.

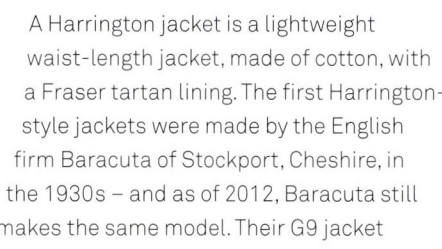

A Harrington jacket is a lightweight waist-length jacket, made of cotton, with a Fraser tartan lining. The first Harrington-style jackets were made by the English firm Baracuta of Stockport, Cheshire, in the 1930s – and as of 2012, Baracuta still makes the same model. Their G9 jacket became known as the Harrington when it was worn by the character Rodney Harrington, played by Ryan O'Neal, in the popular 1960s American soap opera *Peyton Place*. The jacket was also worn by Elvis Presley in his 1958 movie *King Creole*, while actor Steve McQueen was regularly seen sporting his.

The jacket became fashionable in the United Kingdom in the 1960s when it was taken up by both the mods and the skinheads, and then again in the late 1970s and early 1980s when those looks were revived. It remains a style staple across many different subcultures – a true classic.

STYLE

Above **David Bowie in his Thin White Duke period (1976), a look that influenced both Dior and Lanvin. In the lead-up to the major Bowie retrospective at the Victoria and Albert Museum, London, in 2013, many designers were looking to Bowie for inspiration. In what was very much a Zeitgeist moment, his influence was strongly evident in both menswear and womenswear.**

Opposite left **Dior, Spring/Summer 2011, Paris.**

Opposite right **Lanvin, Autumn/Winter 2011, Paris.**

'Style' is that indefinable, enduring thing that means different things to different people – a certain way of dressing, a distinctiveness of appearance. Some individuals have an innate sense of style, a classic, timeless and unchanging personal mode of expression that seems inbuilt and natural. Famous style icons have always been admired and copied by their followers, defining fashions and setting trends.

Developments in the media during the twentieth and early twenty-first centuries led to the extreme celebrity culture that we know today. The well-dressed Hollywood stars of the 1940s – Cary Grant and Frank Sinatra were no strangers to Savile Row – dressed with a formality that, during the general menswear shift in the 1950s, gradually gave way to the casual style that made style heroes of James Dean and Steve McQueen in their blue jeans and bomber jackets.

Rock and pop stars joined movie stars as style heroes during the 1950s, and subcultures, or style tribes, were born from their allegiance with new and different musical genres as much as from the personal style of individual performers and groups.

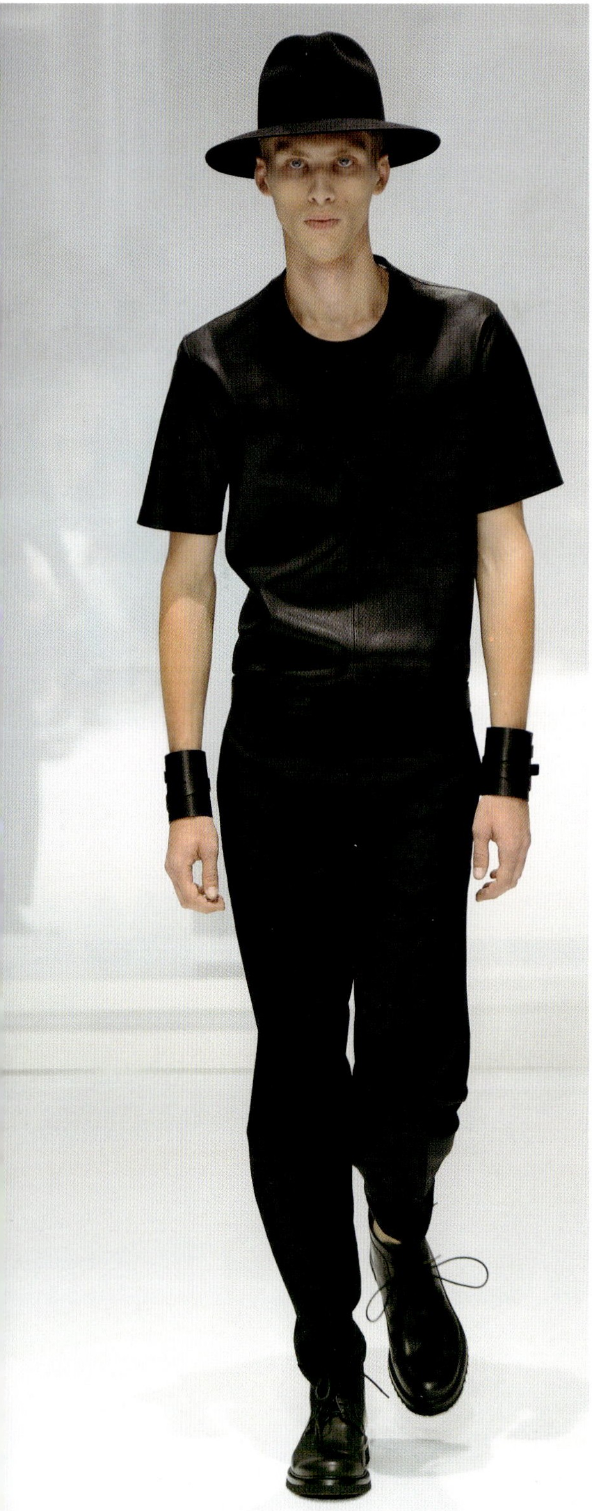

RESEARCH AND INSPIRATION 57

THE DUKE OF WINDSOR

'I was in fact "produced" as a leader of fashion, with the clothiers as my showmen and the world as my audience.'

Edward, Duke of Windsor (1894–1972), was a small man with a large wardrobe: it has been claimed that not since King George IV in the 1820s had a male member of the British royal family lavished so much expense on his personal wardrobe.

Edward reigned briefly as King Edward VIII, but famously abdicated the throne in December 1936 rather than end his relationship with Wallis Simpson (a married American woman who had already been divorced once), which was deemed incompatible with his position as king and head of the Church of England. After the abdication he was given the title Duke of Windsor.

With a reputation as one of the best-dressed men in the world, the Duke found his clothes closely scrutinized and his style imitated worldwide. From 1919 to 1959 he used the same tailor, Scholte of Savile Row, to tailor his jackets, while he had matching trousers made by Harris of New York, preferring the American flat-fronted style of trouser. He always opted for British fabrics, and was particularly fond of Scottish tweeds and Fair Isle sweaters. A 1960 inventory of his wardrobe recorded fifteen evening suits, fifty-five lounge suits and three formal suits (with two pairs of trousers for each), along with more than one hundred pairs of shoes, including a fabulous collection of velvet slippers by English bespoke footwear maker Peal & Co.

Many types of clothing and styles of dress can be credited to the Duke of Windsor, either because he wore them first or because he was responsible for their spread. His visits to the United States were closely followed by the fashion cognoscenti and he inspired several trends there. For example, he revived the wearing of Panama hats by wearing a large Panama hat at Belmont Park, Long Island, where more than 50,000 people saw him. The Windsor knot that he favoured became a standard way to wear a tie, with a large, symmetrical knot worn with a spread collar. The Duke was also known for wearing a tab collar – a collar with a strip that attaches the points to one another under the tie.

In the 1920s the then Prince of Wales visited Fair Isle, off the coast of Scotland, during a period of local economic depression. The island is famous for its colourful, patterned knitwear. After photographs of Edward on the golf links wearing a Fair Isle sweater appeared in newspapers, the crofters were swamped with orders for their hand-knit sweaters, and a trend was sparked in the United States and beyond (see also pp. 130–35).

Another garment that became popular in the United States thanks to the Duke was the Guards overcoat. Similarly, brown buckskin shoes became fashionable after he appeared at a polo

Below Prince Edward, right, on a visit to the Admiralty during the First World War.

Opposite Prince Edward wearing a French beret, Le Bourget Airport, Paris, August 1931.

Above left, above centre and right **The Duke of Windsor on a transatlantic cruise aboard the RMS *Queen Elizabeth*,** c. 1950.

Above right **A young Prince Edward in naval uniform,** c. 1910.

match at Meadow Brook, Long Island, wearing brown buckskin shoes with his chalk-striped flannel suit.

After his abdication, the Duke of Windsor went to live abroad, marrying Wallis Simpson in 1937. He enjoyed frequenting the fashionable resorts of the French Riviera, and many of the various styles of sports shirts and trousers that became popular in the United States were first worn by him there, including the dark-blue linen sports shirt and fisherman's red linen slacks. He remained a source of inspiration to designers and producers of men's clothing, and earned his place as one of the most influential figures in menswear of the twentieth century.

Below **The Duke of Windsor sitting in a chair, smoking his pipe, during a visit to the French Riviera, 1950s.**

POPULAR CULTURE

Zeitgeist means the spirit of the times and can comprise a myriad of elements, whether political, environmental, ecological, economic, musical, scientific or technological. It can include films, natural disasters, social issues, television, pop music and street style. The best designers tap into the Zeitgeist to be in tune with popular culture and aware of the rich and fruitful past. As Belgian fashion designer Walter Van Beirendonck told me: 'I'm permanently researching and looking for new ideas. Rituals, art, ethnic tribes, music, history and historic garments … the world around me is all inspiration.'

For Sharon Graubard of Stylesight, 'film is great source for menswear research and inspiration; every time I watch a film, whether it is a 1920s silent movie with hobos or a police chase movie from the 1970s, I think: Here is a whole collection.'

RESEARCH AND INSPIRATION

Opposite **Buster Keaton and Charlotte Greenwood** guard their golf clubs in *Parlor, Bedroom and Bath* (1931; released in the UK as *Romeo in Pyjamas*), directed by Edward Sedgwick.

Right A Buster Keaton-inspired creation by British designer John Galliano, men's ready-to-wear, Spring/Summer 2011, Paris.

Andrew Groves, course director at the University of Westminster, London, believes in the adaptation of existing customs. 'To be a successful menswear designer,' he says, 'one has to draw on all its traditions and customs and reinvent them, and adapt them to be relevant to what a contemporary modern man desires. Menswear in particular likes to underline a sense of timeless style, but in reality this changes constantly and needs to be relevant to the Zeitgeist and what it means to be a man at any given time in society. Are the ideals and archetypes for men at one particular time about being an adventurer, or businessman, or eco-warrior? A good designer is able to adapt their work to make it seem both contemporary and also timeless.'

HERITAGE

Heritage is associated with the handing down of traditions and, in fashion, a legacy of quality and craftmanship. When used effectively, it can lead to feelings of nostalgia for another time or place and makes for an excellent sales and marketing tool. Brands often play upon their perceived heritage, regardless of whether it is truly genuine or carefully manufactured. Their shared aim is to instill in the target audience or customer a sense of nostalgia that can evoke trust and is associated with days gone by and a feeling of 'better times'.

True heritage brands have long histories and strong back catalogues that can be drawn upon and reinvented to move the brand and its designs forward. Burberry is the perfect example of this type of company: it has a rich history of design output but is still at the forefront of modern fashion, as a result of its innovative use of modern fabrics, manufacturing techniques and, most importantly in its case, new media and technology.

Kim Jones, menswear designer at Louis Vuitton, has talked about how he has always been acutely aware of how steeped in tradition the house is and of the values it stands for: these elements are always at the forefront of his mind while designing.

Some companies, such as Barbour in the United Kingdom and Carhartt in the United States, take pride in their sense of national identity. An appeal to patriotism can be a potent tool: think of Ralph Lauren's advertisements featuring models draped in the Stars and Stripes, or Hackett's rugby shirts with their Union Jacks, or Paul Smith's use of British iconography to promote the Britishness of his brand to the rest of the world.

Abercrombie & Fitch has a long history in sporting goods but only a relatively short history as a sportswear company; it still trades on this imagined long and rich heritage. Jack Wills performs a similar feat in the United Kingdom with its trademark 'University Outfitters'. Founded only in 1999, the label would have us believe it has been around as long as the great universities and colleges themselves. Abercrombie & Fitch and Jack Wills both decorate their stores with trophies and antiques to evoke this mythical sporting heritage.

Fashion may be about the future, but we all very definitely buy into the past.

Opposite **1920s and 1930s sporting clothes and equipment on display at The Vintage Showroom.**

Below: **J. F. K. Hinde, cox of the University of Cambridge rowing crew, inspects one of the boats used in training, March 1952.**

Below right **'Bright Young Things' of the 1920s: socialite Richard Colley and friends pose for a photograph.**

BARBOUR

Barbour began in 1894 when John Barbour, originally of Galloway, Scotland, founded the company in South Shields, England, making coats out of Scottish oilcloth. The UK Admiralty became a customer during the First World War, as did trawlermen, the police force and other outdoor workers, from shepherds to submariners. Today the fifth-generation family-owned business remains in England's Northeast, with Barbour's headquarters located in Simonside, South Shields.

Barbour is renowned for its countrywear, and its classic waxed cotton jackets in autumnal tones were – and indeed still are – favoured by royalty and the country set. Branching out from its countrywear roots, the label gradually gained popularity among the fashion set too, sparking collaborations with Paul Smith, Anya Hindmarch and Amanda Harlech, muse to Karl Lagerfeld at Chanel.

The company remains true to its core values as a family business and describes the Barbour brand as having 'contemporary style inspired by the British countryside, ideal for country and town'. Its rich history in weatherproof clothing is reinvented and updated in its heritage collections; details remain authentic while the cuts and fabrics give a modern twist to the traditional product.

Barbour's motorcycle clothing, which has been produced since 1936, gave rise to its International line, a reworking of traditional motorcycle jackets in modern fabrications. In 2013 the label introduced the Steve McQueen Collection, referencing the most stylish of style icons and a former customer of its motorcycle jackets.

Above **Classic waxed Barbour jacket with checked lining.**

Opposite **Field-style Barbour jacket.**

C. P. COMPANY/ AITOR THROUP

Aitor Throup's development sketches for his reworking of the Mille Miglia Goggle Jacket.

Originally designed in 1988 by Massimo Osti for the thousand-mile Italian open-road endurance race, the Mille Miglia, C. P. Company's Goggle Jacket has become a staple garment for the brand, with redesigns by Osti, Moreno Ferrari and Alessandro Pungetti utilizing new advances in fabrics and fabric treatments coming out of the company's research lab.

To celebrate the twentieth anniversary of the jacket's first release C.P. Company invited Aitor Throup, a graduate of London's Royal College of Art, to reinvent this iconic piece.

Explaining his design on C. P. Company's website, Throup says: 'The Goggle Jacket is the reason I became a designer. Back in Burnley where I (partly) grew up it was a cultural icon utilized almost as a status symbol. What the Goggle Jacket did for me was open a door to the world of design. I became more aware and passionate about brands such as C. P. Company, Stone Island ... and, of course, Massimo Osti Production. The Goggle Jacket taught and formed me, and through my studies I strove to replicate an approach to design which could equal the precision and integrity of what I considered (and still consider) to be the pinnacle of design.'

The original jacket was designed to be functional for endurance motoring. The goggles built into the hood of the jacket and the plastic 'window' on the left sleeve, through which the driver can look at his watch, have become iconic design features synonymous with the brand.

'The basis of my approach,' says Throup, 'has been to take Osti's classic back to the race itself.' He redesigned the jacket on a human model in a seated driving position, so the sleeves are pitched forwards and bent and the lower part of the jacket morphs from a standing position into a more complex driving position, which eliminates excess bunching and provides a cover for the legs. The hood was completely reconstructed to be anatomically correct with the ability to fit over a driving helmet when the drawstrings are loosened. The accompanying gloves provide a better wheel grip, while a detachable pouch can hold cameras and phones so they might easily be reached while driving.

The fabric of the jacket is a three-layer Gore-Tex performance shell fabric with a waterproof membrane, with each seam finished with waterproof thermo-taping. The garment is hand-dyed using the company's signature technique of colouring with natural derivatives from different-coloured soils, their place of origin defining the colours and rendering each garment unique.

Below **The Goggle Jacket** photographed in standing and seated (driving) position.

Right **The Goggle Jacket** and its component parts.

BELSTAFF

The bastion of British motorcycle clothing, Belstaff was founded in Longton, Staffordshire, in 1924 by Eli Belovitch and his son-in-law Harry Grosberg. It originally produced all-weather jackets for motorcyclists and was the first ever company to use waxed cotton. It diversified to produce weather-protective jackets for other uses, goggles (primarily for the growing aviation market), gloves and several other garments intended to keep the wearer warm and dry.

Perhaps Belstaff's most famous garment is the Trialmaster jacket. First produced in 1948, it became an instant favourite among motorcycle enthusiasts. Ernesto 'Che' Guevara wore an early version of it on his famous motorcycle expeditions through South America in the early 1950s, providing him security and protection as he travelled through the vast continent's many different climates.

That iconic creation has now inspired a series of jackets, each with its own unique heritage, collectively known as the Legends Collection. With the motorcyclist in mind, each piece is designed with the same practical and utilitarian elements that made the Trialmaster such an iconic piece. These jackets form the foundation of the Belstaff business which, since being acquired by the Labelux Group in 2011, has propelled itself on to the international fashion scene, showing twice yearly in Milan and establishing itself as a luxury brand. Martin Cooper, who had worked at Burberry for sixteen years, was appointed as chief creative officer.

'As soon as I was hired,' Cooper said to Susannah Frankel in *W* magazine in September 2012, 'I wanted to take ownership of certain icons.' The rubber Despatch Rider coat has undergone a transformation to forest-green PVC bonded to neoprene, while the four-pocket Trialmaster will be offered in luxurious skins such as crocodile and python.

Below Vintage Belstaff advertisements showing the brand's core product.

Opposite left Vintage Belstaff Trialmaster at The Vintage Showroom.

Opposite right Reinvention of the classic Trialmaster jacket, Belstaff, Autumn/Winter 2013.

RESEARCH AND INSPIRATION 71

WORLD

Almost all cultures around the world have some form of traditional dress or folk costume. It is usually an indicator of religion, status or social standing, and is more often than not worn for special occasions.

Places in the world still exist where it is a legal requirement to wear traditional dress; one of those is Bhutan, the destination of Kim Jones for his research trip for the Louis Vuitton Men Autumn/Winter 2013 collection. There, a law requires government employees to wear national dress for work and all other Bhutanese citizens to wear national dress while visiting schools and government offices. Many Bhutanese choose to wear this traditional dress for formal occasions.

Bhutanese textiles are based on geometric grid formations and inspired by sacred iconography and beliefs; Jones took these textiles as inspiration for his own custom checked and striped cloths used for luxury duffel coats and ponchos.

Paris-based fashion designer Damir Doma is well known for bringing cultural references into his collections, as is John Galliano, also based in Paris. Doma was described on Style.com as having 'exported his sensibility to the corners of the globe, drawing on African, Slavic and Asian costumes',

Opposite left **Yohji Yamamoto's Autumn/Winter 2011 collection, featuring his signature nineteenth-century-inspired tailoring.**

Opposite right **Portrait of Thomas Howey wearing an asymmetrically fastening jacket, 1873.**

Below **A Mongolian man makes a freezing winter migration.**

Right **John Galliano, Autumn/Winter 2011.**

in the review for his Autumn/Winter 2012 catwalk presentation, which saw ikat patterns mixed with flowing robes, kimonos and shaggy fur gilets.

Belgian designer Dries Van Noten is also well known for his masterly use of textiles of all kinds. He deftly mixes rich brocades with different types of lace and uses Asian and African themes for rich prints and weaves inspired by ikat textiles and other traditional fabrics from many cultures and places.

Men's fashion inspired by traditional clothing can, of course, feature elements other than brightly coloured prints, ethnic patterns and outlandish accessories: it might be something as subtle as the wrap of a Japanese kimono or the cut of a Thai fisherman's trousers.

Inspiration comes in many forms and it is up to the designer to choose carefully from the melting pot to create his or her own vision.

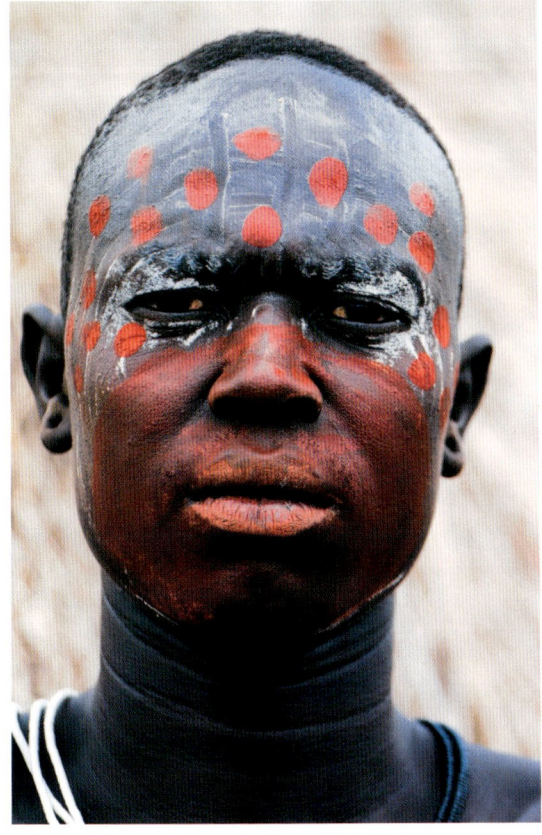

Right Portrait of Mursi man with face paint, South Omo Valley, Ethiopia.

Left A Child of the Jago, Spring/Summer 2013.

Opposite Walter Van Beirendonck, Autumn/Winter 2011.

CASE STUDY
KELVIN KWOK, CENTRAL SAINT MARTINS, LONDON

Kelvin Kwok of Central Saint Martins, London, found inspiration in the waste left behind by the coffee industry when designing his 2013 BA graduate collection. His research materials are shown on these pages.

'With its distinct aroma and flavour, coffee is one of the world's most widely consumed beverages. According to some studies, cultivation of the coffee seed originated in Ethiopia in approximately AD 850, and under the effect of navigation and the discovery of new lands across the oceans by Portugal and Spain, the farming of the coffee plant was introduced by Europeans to the Caribbean and South America in the sixteenth and seventeeth centuries. It was discovered that the land and weather in those areas, primarily in equatorial Latin America, not only was suitable for the plantation of coffee plants, but could also give birth to an even better type of coffee bean. Coffee beans became a major cash crop and an important export product for developing nations such as Brazil, Mexico and Peru. Latin America is now responsible for approximately forty-five per cent of the world's total coffee exports.

'According to the "Total Production of Exporting Countries" published by the International Coffee Organization in April 2012, the number of bags of coffee exported by Brazil alone in 2010 was 48,095,000. Arising from such huge consumption, a large amount of coffee bags left behind will be considered wastage. My final year study attempted to turn such "waste" into a value-added commodity by evoking the concept of fashion design.

'Inspired by the above, I selected some countries in South America to be my main subject for design study and concept development. All of these countries have similar historical backgrounds to that of my home town, Hong Kong, in their rather long experiences of colonialism, but at the same time each retains a strong sense of native culture. My research and study concentrated on three aspects: colonial influence, native cultural characteristics and contemporary development. My work tried to fuse the three elements together, interwoven with my own interpretation of modern fashion (menswear) techniques, in order to spark new understandings of "antiquated vs. new" and "native vs. foreign". The outcome of such a mixture subsequently evoked deep-rooted effects on my design and inspiration.'

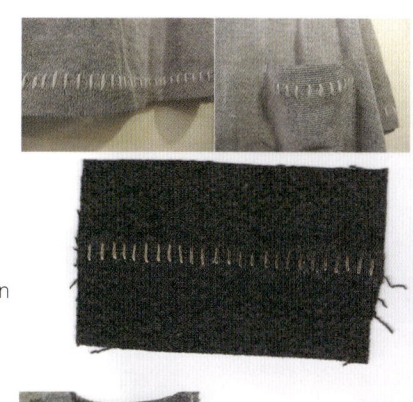

jacket coat

AMF stitch
(off tone thread)

AMF stitch
(off tone thread)

Conceal Bottons

2 Bottons

curve in ??

pocket flip

Stencil print

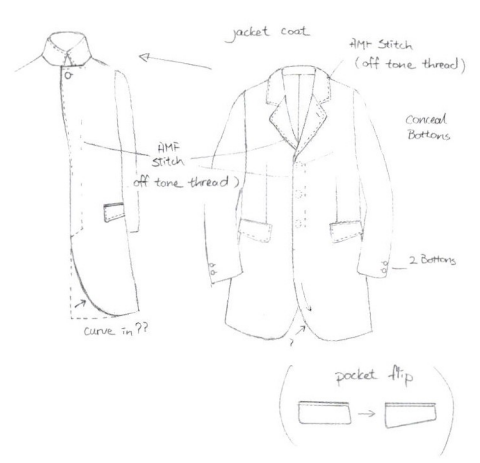

stripes

FORMAL WEAR

Formal wear follows a set of strict rules that have changed little over the decades. Black tie is the gold standard for formal occasions and comprises a black wool jacket with satin or grosgrain facings (with either a peaked or a shawl collar), teamed with trousers that should have matching side stripes and no turn-ups. A wing collar is worn for the more formal white-tie event, but for black-tie events a regular turned-down collar is preferable.

Perhaps the largest sartorial change in twentieth-century formal wear was the introduction by the then Prince of Wales (later Duke of Windsor; see pp. 58–61) of the white marcella (piqué) waistcoat worn with a black dinner jacket. Prior to 1919, this combination had not been seen in either the United Kingdom or the United States, but after the Prince of Wales substituted the white waistcoat others soon followed his lead, including King Alfonso XIII of Spain and well-dressed Americans who were frequent visitors to London, such as the socialite Anthony Joseph Drexel Biddle and the financier William Goadby Loew. The style spread to the United States, until by the mid- to late 1920s black evening waistcoats were seldom seen on better-dressed men.

Formal-wear-inspired moodboard by Goioiza Ferreras Gandiaga, University of Westminster, London.

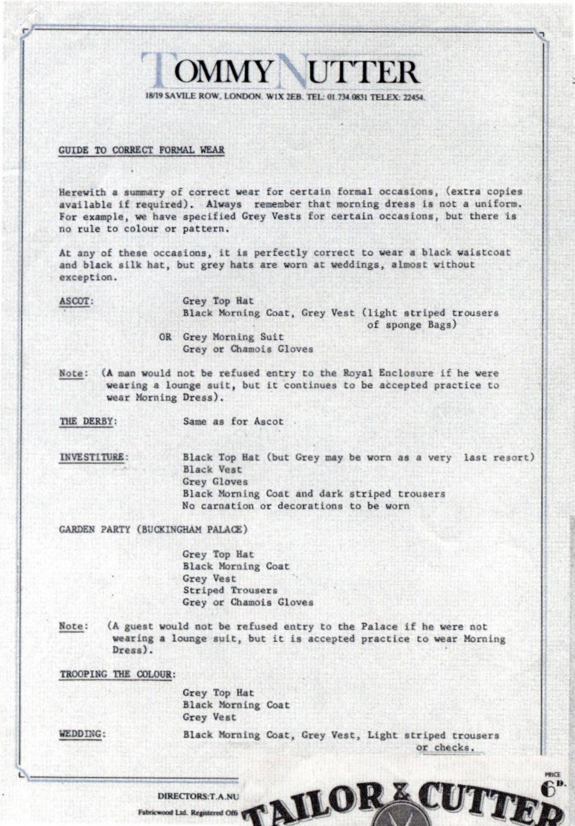

Top Tommy Nutter guide to formal wear, as given to customers, 1980s.

Inset left Cover of *Tailor & Cutter* featuring formal wear, 1945.

Inset right Formal-wear illustration from *Tailor & Cutter*, 1952.

Dress rules exist for all sorts of occasions, including weddings, funerals, the races, investitures or the Trooping of the Colour. They dictate details such as which colour of trouser to wear with what jacket, right down to the correct choice of hat, shoes and waistcoat.

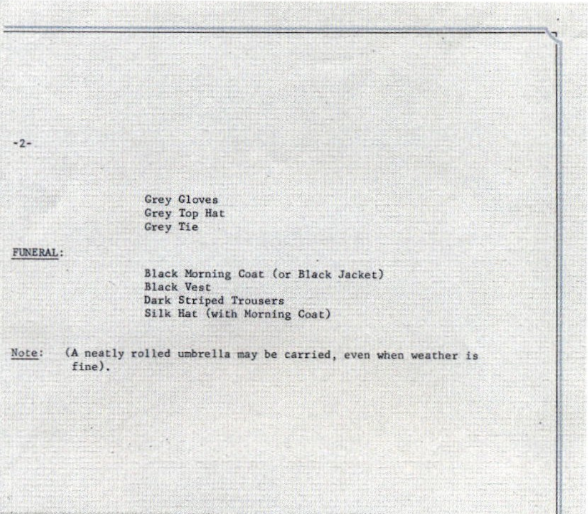

Dylan Jones, editor of *GQ* magazine, says: 'Designers will always try and reinvent formal wear, which is obviously their right. However the great thing about formal wear is that it is a uniform and really shouldn't be messed with.'

When asked what advice he would give to the well-dressed man regarding formal wear, he replied simply: 'Don't experiment.'

SAVILE ROW

Since the early nineteenth century, tailors have operated from Savile Row, in London's Mayfair, attracted at first by the wealthy local clientele, many of whom had military connections. The term 'bespoke' is said to have originated there. Throughout its history, Savile Row has had customers from kings to movie stars and has earned a worldwide reputation as the spiritual home of men's tailoring.

The first-ever dinner jacket was made on Savile Row in 1865 by Henry Poole for 'Bertie', Prince of Wales (later King Edward VII). Gieves dressed the legendary British explorer David Livingstone for his 1866 expedition to find the source of the Nile; and the journalist H. M. Stanley, sent to look for Livingstone in 1869, was dressed by Henry Poole.

Anderson & Sheppard clothed Rudolph Valentino during the 1920s, along with Noël Coward – and made Marlene Dietrich's trouser suits; it still enjoys the patronage of Prince Charles to this day.

Hollywood mogul Louis B. Mayer selected Kilgour, French & Stanbury as his tailor of choice, as did David Niven and Frank Sinatra. In 1959 the tailor created Cary Grant's suits for Alfred Hitchcock's *North by Northwest*, and later dressed 1960s style icon Michael Caine in his cult movie *The Italian Job* (1969). In 2003 the renamed Kilgour appointed Carlo Brandelli as creative director to grow the ready-to-wear side of the business.

Savile Row was very much part of the establishment when, in 1969, Tommy Nutter caused a quiet revolution with the opening of his first

Savile Row-inspired mood board by Jack Byne, University of Westminster, London.

Savile Row-inspired mood board by Yasemin Calki, University of Westminster, London.

shop, Nutters, which left its windows open to the street, unlike all the other tailors, and brought in a rock-star clientele. Following in Nutter's footsteps, several new tailors opened for business in Savile Row, bringing a younger, more fashion-conscious customer to the Row with modern cuts and fabrics, and recognizable house styles. These included Richard James in 1992, followed in 1994 by Ozwald Boateng. In 2005 entrepreneur Patrick Grant acquired Norton & Son.

In 2007 Italian fashion foundation Pitti Immagine Uomo commissioned the first major exhibition dedicated to Savile Row's bespoke tailoring, 'The London Cut'. The exhibition ran for a month, with an accompanying book written by its curator James Sherwood. The Chambre Syndicale de la Haute Couture invited Savile Row to bring 'The London Cut' to the British Ambassador's residence in Paris during July Couture Week.

Reinforcing the fact that it has gained recognition in the field of fashion, for London's Men's Fashion Week in January 2013, Savile Row's finest joined forces for a presentation at Spencer House named 'The English Gentlemen', and showed their skills alongside the British menswear designers.

Dylan Jones, editor of *GQ* and chair of London Collections: Men, comments: 'I think there is such a wealth of great tailoring talent in the UK at present, including the great heritage Savile Row designers as well as the new breed of designers who take British tailoring so seriously. London is the home of menswear, and it's never been so apparent as it is now.'

CASE STUDY
LAURENS BRUNT, AMSTERDAM FASHION INSTITUTE (AMFI)

Laurens Brunt of the Amsterdam Fashion Institute found inspiration in print and printing techniques when designing his graduate collection. The research materials in his sketchbook are shown here.

'These images come from the workbook of my graduation collection, in which the emphasis was on prints. I made a fictional collection for the Paul Smith brand, whereby I tried to define a new approach to prints and patterns for traditional or formal menswear which is the essence of the brand: classic menswear with a twist.

'Inspiration came from the idea that we've accepted the illusions that come with embracing digital up to a point that we don't even notice it any more: like not being able to look each other directly in the eye when talking over Skype. I researched in modern art, where I found various artists playing around with the idea of optical illusion.

'I also did a lot of research on printing techniques; printing stripes with flock-ink over existing striped suit fabrics. I used digital printing in different sizes on various materials and experimented with patterned cutouts to show the lining through the fabric of a dinner jacket.'

RESEARCH AND INSPIRATION 83

GARMENT CASE STUDY
BLAZER STRIPES

This page Advertisements for 'Striped Blazers' and 'Caps and Badges For All Sports', 1920s; Edwardian gentlemen in blazers and linens enjoy a camping trip, England.

Opposite, clockwise from left Dries Van Noten, Autumn/Winter 2010; Edwardian cricketer in striped blazer; 1920s sporting blazer at The Vintage Showroom.

STRIPED BLAZERS

Club striped Tennis and Cricket Blazers. These are always available in a wide range of colours and various width stripes. Practically any particular combination can be secured at short notice.

READY-FOR-SERVICE

In all fittings ... **29/6**

CAPS AND BADGES FOR ALL SPORTS

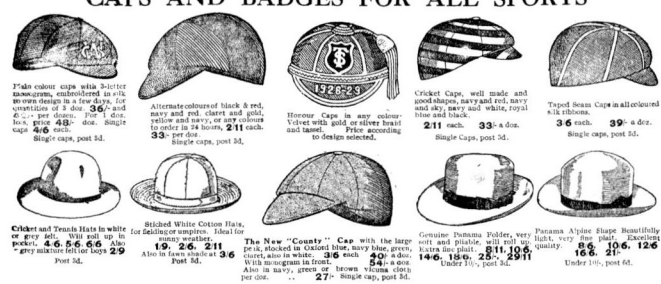

A.E. Stoddart

GIEVES & HAWKES

Above **Gieves coachman livery of the Earl of Dudley, nineteenth century.**

Opposite **Images from the Gieves & Hawkes exhibition at Spencer House, 2013.**

When we consider that Gieves dressed Lord Nelson and that Hawkes dressed the Duke of Wellington, we begin to get some sense of just how incredible a history the military tailor Gieves & Hawkes has.

James Gieve began his training as a tailor in 1835 under Melchisedek Meredith, who ran a tailoring business in Portsmouth. It was Meredith who had tailored the uniform that Admiral Lord Nelson was wearing when killed in action at the Battle of Trafalgar.

After Meredith's death in 1841, James Galt took over the business and Gieve became a partner in 1852. Gieve bought out Galt in 1887 to establish Gieves & Co., and following his death in 1888 his two sons, James W. Gieve and John Gieve, took over the business. In 1900, at a time when more than half of the world's shipping was controlled by Britain, Gieves became tailor by appointment to the Royal Navy. Being dressed by 'the man from Gieves' became an integral part of being a cadet at the Royal Naval College. The company received a Royal Warrant from King George V in 1911.

During the Second World War the company was commissioned to create buttons concealing maps, razor wire and suicide pills for British agents crossing enemy lines. When Queen Elizabeth celebrated her coronation in 1953, interest in ceremonial tailoring was reignited; Gieves created a boat cloak for Her Majesty, which is still worn today but now tailored for Prince Philip.

The history of Hawkes is just as interesting. Thomas Hawkes started in the tailoring business as an apprentice to a velvet hat maker in London's Soho in 1771, but soon set up on his own. He received a Royal Warrant of Appointment to King George III and Queen Charlotte in 1809. After the death of Hawkes the company continued in business and in 1837 the Duke of Wellington ordered ceremonial uniforms for both his personal wardrobe and his regiments. In 1840 Prince Albert, newly married to Queen Victoria, ordered caps to be made for his regiment, Prince Albert's Own 11th Hussars. Hawkes & Co. earned the Royal Warrants of Prince Albert and Queen Victoria.

Hawkes bought Number 1 Savile Row in 1912. During the 1920s the demand for ready-to-wear clothing steadily grew and Hawkes & Co. became one of the first on the Row to introduce what it called 'Immediate Wear', a move that was to sustain its business during a decline in the popularity of bespoke clothing.

1974 saw Gieves and Hawkes merge into one company, Gieves & Hawkes, located at the prestigious address Number 1 Savile Row. In the twenty-first century, the company is a leading supplier of the finest quality traditional and contemporary menswear. Some of its wonderful archive, which includes past commissions, pictures and documentation, is available for the public to view in the first-floor gallery of the Savile Row shop; the company draws on this fascinating resource to this day.

TOMMY NUTTER

Born in 1943, Tommy Nutter trained at London's renowned Tailor & Cutter Academy in the early 1960s and then spent several years at the tailor Donaldson, Williamson & Ward. He is best remembered for bringing fashion to Savile Row, together with Edward Sexton, with the opening of his first shop, Nutters of Savile Row, in 1969. With this shop he attracted a new and different clientele to Savile Row – the rock and pop stars of the day. He also opened up the traditionally closed and dark frontage to reveal the interior of the store. Savile Row had seen nothing like it: the bastion of traditional British menswear was shaken.

One of Nutter's business backers was Peter Brown, an executive of The Beatles' Apple Corps, whose headquarters was also in Savile Row.

The Beatles became regular customers, as did Mick Jagger of The Rolling Stones; he and Bianca Jagger were married in 1971 wearing matching white suits tailored by Nutters.

On splitting with Sexton, Nutter was licensed through Austin Reed and had successful business dealings with the Far East. Nutter returned to the Row in 1983 with a ready-to-wear store, Tommy Nutter, at number 19. The large double-fronted shop was furnished with a mixture of antiques and modern design classics. From here Nutter continued to dress his clientele of the rich, famous and discerning, enjoying the patronage of, among many others, shoemaker Manolo Blahnik and musician Elton John (for whom he made many of his famous stage costumes). John Galliano spent some time interning there during his college days and delighted Nutter with his stylish window displays. Timothy Everest, one of the brightest stars of the current London tailoring scene, also cut his teeth at number 19.

Cited as influential by everyone from Tom Ford to Vivienne Westwood, Nutter was celebrated for his influence on modern menswear with an exhibition at the Fashion and Textiles Museum in London in 2011. This introduced the signature Nutter look to a new generation – that unmistakable dash of the Roaring Twenties, teamed with the strong, square shoulders of the 1940s, all skilfully melded into thoroughly modern menswear, and at the same time always immediately recognizable as Nutter.

All images from the Tommy Nutter exhibition at the Fashion and Textiles Museum, London, 2011.

TIMOTHY EVEREST

Welsh-born Timothy Everest started his career in Savile Row during the late 1980s working for Tommy Nutter. On leaving the Row he set up business in London's East End, finding premises in one of the beautiful Georgian houses of Spitalfields once inhabited by Huguenot silk weavers. Passionate about quality but ambivalent about the stuffiness of Savile Row at that time, he set about building a business for a new breed of bespoke customer, from art dealers to hedge fund managers.

Everest describes his customers as 'people who've gone beyond the dictates of high fashion and want a modern, invigorated and not-too-reverent take on contemporary tailoring. And they push our boundaries as often as we push theirs.'

Building the business to become more than just a bespoke tailoring service, Everest looked to different areas of menswear, including such garments as pea coats and cycling jackets, and bringing bespoke tailoring techniques to bear on these less formal garments.

Aside from his core business, Everest worked with DAKS as group creative director from 2000 to 2003, and was responsible for the global restructuring of the classic British company. For the past decade, he has acted as creative consultant for Marks & Spencer, overseeing the Autograph, Sartorial and Luxury tailoring collections. He also has an on-going role as creative contributor and style arbiter for luxe gents' style bible *The Rake*.

As of 2013 Everest had teamed up with iconic British fashion company Superdry to design an exclusive collection of contemporary British tailoring. The range, which is called Sebiro (Japanese for suit), comprises a collection of core wardrobe staples with youthful super-skinny cuts and fine-quality fabrics. Designed as separates to mix and match with Superdry's existing casual pieces, the range centres around four key inspirational characters – Super Spy, Bank Robber, San Franciscan and Country Rebel – each with its own defining stylistic traits.

Above **Portrait of Timothy Everest.**

Right **Cutting a yellow Melton undercollar at the Timothy Everest atelier, Spitalfields, London.**

RESEARCH AND INSPIRATION   91

Above Soft construction jacket, featuring cloth designed by Yangzi Wang and woven by Fox Brothers & Co. Single-breasted three-button jacket with on-the-turn notch lapel featuring quilted Melton undercollar and red flower loop.

Right Timothy Everest Bespoke Casual soft construction single-breasted donkey jacket fashioned from W. Bill worsted with jewel-like flecks. Featuring contrasting yoke, extended elbow patch, tab cuffs, storm collar piece, patch pockets and buggy half-lining with bound internal seams.

UNIFORM

Uniform, in all its guises, is one of the richest areas of research for menswear. It has it all, from built-in functionality and inherent masculinity, to rich detailing, colour and sturdy construction methods, not to mention its sheer diversity. Uniform has developed and evolved over the centuries for reasons of recognition, function and effect.

Although different armed forces have different attitudes to their kit, former soldier and military anthropologist Dr Charles Kirke writes: 'A highly valued element of looking "soldierly" is to be convincing; to cut the right figure, his military clothing and equipment had to fit properly and he had to wear it in a soldierly way. This went beyond the simply utilitarian. At various times I have seen … "creases" sewn down the front of combat pants to make them appear pressed, or light cotton jungle rags used as neck cloths in chilly European winters to show the wearer had jungle experience.'

From rugged military combat gear, with its functional pockets and detailing as well as its insignia, to the prints of camouflage and the more

Below An American soldier in uniform stands surrounded by other pieces of his military outfit, 1942.

Opposite top First World War portrait of two men in their respective army and navy uniforms.

Opposite bottom Military-tailoring-inspired mood board by Christopher Pak, University of Westminster, London.

RESEARCH AND INSPIRATION 93

1918 Henry Poole Military Jacket.

US Army M 1942 Parachute Jump Jacket

double sided knife pocket

exuberant ceremonial military uniforms, there is something in all of these elements to inspire the designer.

A great many garment types familiar to menswear are based on military pieces and have now entered mainstream fashion. Certain garments have become favourites for particular designers and brands to rework, such as the field jacket at Stone Island, the trench coat at Burberry and Raf Simons's signature cold-weather parkas.

COMBAT KIT

Main picture **Junya Watanabe, Autumn/Winter 2006.** Inspired by military garments, the parka and the MA1 jacket were both reworked by Watanabe.

Left **US Marine Sergeant, New Orleans, during the Second World War.**

Below **British soldiers from a Scottish regiment wearing khaki kilt covers, Jerusalem, 1936.**

Bottom **An American soldier on a street in Columbus, Georgia, USA, 1941.**

TROPICAL UNIFORM

Uniforms have often had to adapt for many reasons, including those of camouflage, status and practicality. Colonialism and warfare overseas in warmer climates saw the more usual woollen battle dress replaced by lighter, more practical cotton fabrics suited to the heat. Olive greens were re-coloured to khaki and a lighter, sand-coloured khaki for reasons of camouflage.

Hawkes (which merged with Gieves in 1974 to become Gieves & Hawkes; see pp.86–87) patented its solar topi in 1867. A cork-lined helmet originally designed to protect military men from the sun, it was soon taken up for civilian dress and is more usually known nowadays as a pith helmet.

Above right Two Victorian gentlemen pose in solar topis for their portrait in Bombay, India, 1890s.

Right Prince Edward, far left, dressed for tropical weather in a lightweight suit and pith helmet, East Africa, 1928.

Opposite, clockwise from top Solar topis on display at the Gieves & Hawkes archive; Jean Paul Gaultier suit inspired by tropical uniform, Spring/Summer 2011; tropical kit on display at the Gieves & Hawkes archive.

CASE STUDY
AARON TUBB, UNIVERSITY OF WESTMINSTER, LONDON

Aaron Tubb's graduate collection was inspired by the Russian 'gopnik' subculture, which is defined by its aggression and football fanaticism. He was drawn to these youths by their eclectic mix of sportswear and formal wear – their uniform of dress shoes with white tube socks and track pants is an unexpected mix to the Western fashion eye.

For his silhouettes, Tubb deconstructed carefully selected army surplus from around the globe, extensively researching the jackets of the world's military for details and shapes.

Taking these pieces, he scanned and photocopied them life-size, then collaged them to redefine and reinvent them, drawing into them and coming up with endless variations to choose from for his final designs.

Aware that menswear operates within strict parameters and historical codes, Tubb took the manliest of garments – the army uniform – and reimagined it for the street in sportswear fabrics intended to appeal to the contemporary menswear consumer.

Aaron Tubb of the University of Westminster, London, took inspiration from the Russian 'gopnik' subculture for his BA graduate collection. His research materials and collection are shown here.

STONE ISLAND

Stone Island was formed in 1982 by Massimo Osti as a sister company to his successful C. P. Company (see pp. 68–69). Its design ethos was to take military garments Osti had sourced from second-hand markets for his archive and apply the brand's innovative fabric and manufacturing techniques to bring them up to date and make them a desirable product.

Osti was drawn both to the inherent functionality of these garments and to the way the fabrics had worn and aged. In order to reproduce the antique look of his archival pieces he set up and developed a sophisticated garment-dyeing laboratory and experimental printworks in Ravarino, in the province of Modena, Italy. Research began into fabric dyeing and treatments and the weaving process; fabrics were coated and dyed to produce the desired effects.

A particular industrial tarpaulin fabric, double-faced in red and blue, was stonewashed for hours to soften it and make it suitable for clothing manufacture, and it was from this fabric, which was dubbed Tela Stella, that a small range of seven jackets was made – the first of what would be his new brand: Stone Island.

Though born out of Osti's research into army surplus pieces, Stone Island also has a maritime feel, the fabrics reminiscent of oilskins that have been washed and worn down. The logo consists of a compass rose that is displayed like a military insignia, referencing Osti's many archival pieces of military clothing collected over the years.

Below and overleaf **'Stone Island Archivio '982-'012' exhibition, Milan, 2012.**

Opposite **Stone Island field jacket, Spring/Summer 2012, in a highly reflective fabric with a coating made of glass micro-spheres. The finished garments are individually hand-sprayed and then oven-dried.**

CAMOUFLAGE

The first military use of camouflage in a printed form was in the early twentieth century; before this soldiers 'camouflaged' their uniforms by dirtying them with earth.

At the beginning of the First World War in 1914, a specialist camouflage section was set up by the French, which employed hundreds of artists and civilians, known as *camoufleurs*. In 1916 Britain followed the lead of France and started a camouflage section with Solomon J. Solomon, a prolific artist and illustrator of the day, as key adviser; its first camouflage overalls, a sniper suit, went into production in 1918.

Since artists were at the heart of its development, the design of camouflage shifted from an originally Impressionistic style to one much more influenced by Cubism – even this functional military technique being subject to the vagaries of design and fashion.

Designed to mislead rather than conceal, 'Dazzle' camouflage was used on ships. In 1919 the Chelsea Arts Club held a Dazzle Ball at the Royal Albert Hall: partygoers in camouflage costumes danced beneath balloons painted to look like bombs in what was probably the first documented appearance of camouflage being worn as fashionable dress.

In 1939, with the onset of the Second World War, the British Surrealist artist Roland Penrose was commissioned to write *The Home Guard Manual of Camouflage* and became involved with the army's Camouflage Development and Training Centre.

By the early 1960s, camouflage began to be replaced by plain-coloured suits. However, it was to reappear later in the decade, and by 1972 had once again become universal army issue. The American-developed 'chocolate chip' desert camouflage was to become the signature camouflage of the Gulf War of 1990–91, re-emerging as issue for the Iraqi army following the American invasion of 2003.

Aside from the military, camouflage took on a political stance when it was adopted by anti-war protesters in the 1970s. Utilitarian and functional, it then filtered into mainstream streetwear, popular types being British DPM (disruptive pattern material), American desert chocolate chip and woodland, and red Swiss Leibermuster.

Taking their cue from the streets, designers appropriated camouflage for the catwalk, with almost every fashion house or brand using it in some form since that time.

Left and opposite bottom
Vintage camouflage field jackets.

Opposite top **Carhartt WIP Camo jacket.**

Left **Stone Island hand-painted camouflage field jacket, Autumn/Winter 2008.**

Below **Dries Van Noten, Spring/Summer 2013.**

Opposite **Research sketchbook images by Aaron Tubb, University of Westminster, London.**

CEREMONIAL UNIFORM

'I have put on so much of the soldier with my red coat.'
Richard Steele, *The Lying Lover*, 1703

In 1645, during the English Civil War, Oliver Cromwell's Parliament passed laws standardizing military uniforms, making the red coat standard attire for what was collectively known as the New Model Army. Different regiments were identified by the distinctive coloured facings, collars and cuffs of their jackets. Red dyes were inexpensive and easy to obtain at this time. Red coats had been seen in uniforms before this date, most notably in Tudor times (1485–1603), when they were worn by both the Yeoman of the Guard and the King's Lifeguard.

Changes in warfare and battle tactics subsequently made camouflaged uniform more desirable. Red coats made the soldier an easy target, and the red coat was sidelined. It is still worn today for military weddings and ceremonial and state occasions – as well as serving to provide inspiration for designers.

Opposite left Ceremonial-uniform-inspired mood board by Connie Blackaller, University of Westminster, London.

Opposite right A Child of the Jago military-inspired jacket, Spring/Summer 2010.

Above Ceremonial-uniform-inspired mood board by Tascha Elliott, University of Westminster, London.

Right Hawkes Coldstream Guards bandsman's tunic and drum, early twentieth-century.

WORKWEAR

Workwear, literally speaking, is anything worn for work, but the workwear that inspires designers is clothing that was developed to be fit for purpose and has inherent functionality, whether it be an American railroad driver's cap or a nineteenth-century European butcher's apron.

It is the way these items of clothing have evolved over the years to suit their purpose that makes them such a rich source of inspiration for the designer – the way garments are cut for function, as well as the details and the construction methods themselves. Things might be double- or even triple-stitched for sturdiness or riveted for strength, and have pockets or hanging loops in unexpected places that serve to hold tools and equipment.

There is probably no menswear brand that has not at some point turned to workwear for inspiration; for some it is their lifeblood. Carhartt WIP, the European arm of American workwear giant Carhartt, specializes in taking workwear staples and adapting them for the fashion market.

Daiki Suzuki of New York's Engineered Garments sources vintage garments and reinvents them: 'I try to choose good dynamic designs with patterns that can be modified... Usually I rework the fits as lightly as possible, being careful not to (merely) reproduce vintage designs – adding some things and taking some off, balancing it out to make it look new.'

Junya Watanabe is another who frequently refers to workwear for his designs, as well as targeting brands for collaboration. In his Spring/Summer 2006 'Re-constructed Workwear' collection, he joined with the American L. C. King Manufacturing Company. The company was founded in 1913 by Landon Clayton King and manufactures bib overalls, coveralls, carpenter jeans, hunting apparel and denim work coats under the Pointer brand.

Japanese brand Post O'Alls, or Post Overalls, the brainchild of designer Takeshi Ohfuchi, debuted in 1993, aiming to create vintage-inspired but new work clothes that could equal the beautifully made originals.

One of the largest workwear-based areas of menswear is, of course, denim. The main protagonists in that field, both old and new, are discussed in the following pages.

Opposite left **American lumber company worker with apron and tools**, date unknown.

Opposite right **German petrol seller**, c. 1920.

Below **German or Russian butcher**, c. 1920.

Below right **American worker in work coat and tattered trousers**, date unknown.

Main image, right
Rag & Bone denim dungarees, Spring/Summer 2011.

Inset Vintage workwear advertisement.

Below Group of farm workers, Yorkshire, England, c. 1900.

Opposite, clockwise from top Workwear-inspired mood board by Alexander McGrady, University of Westminster, London; Radiator Mine, Mount Pleasant, Pennsylvania, 1936; a farmer at Chicot Farms, Arkansas, striking a match on the button of his overalls, 1939; Dolce & Gabbana, Autumn/Winter 2010.

DENIM

The cloth we know today as denim was originally a sturdy serge fabric made in the French town of Nîmes (hence the word 'denim' – *serge de Nîmes*). The first fabric to be known as 'jean' was an indigo-dyed cotton cloth from the Italian city of Genoa (*Gênes* in French). By the eighteenth century much of this cloth was produced in Lancashire, in the north of England.

Whatever its beginnings, the garments and the trousers made from denim, initially as workwear for railway workers, farmers, builders and the like, were to become a pivotal part of almost every youth movement of the second half of the twentieth century, from skinheads and rockers to punks and hippies. Later, the young adopted jeans as everyday wear, much in the way they did the biker jacket, the T-shirt and, more recently, active sportswear.

By the 1960s denim manufacturers had caught on to the fashionability of their product, and styles were altered and decorated to suit the trends of the day. Denim remained a strong seller during the 1970s, and in the 1980s fashion designers such as Gucci, Calvin Klein and Gloria Vanderbilt started designing and producing own-label jeans. Designer denim was born.

In the early 1990s the youth market largely abandoned denim, replacing jeans with combat trousers and track pants as wardrobe staples. This downturn in the market led to Levi's closing eleven factories, but jeans were to make a come-back by the late 1990s with a new fashion product – 'engineered' jeans.

By 2000 denim was firmly on the fashion map and included in many designer collections. It remains a fashion staple in numerous incarnations, including bleached, raw, distressed, studded and embroidered.

Below **Striped denim work jacket and American engine driver's cap.**

Below right **Workwear display at The Vintage Showroom.**

Opposite **Workwear-inspired mood board by Philip Luu, University of Westminster, London.**

Inset **A group of workers aged as young as ten or eleven, Lawrence, Massachusetts, September 1911.**

Alexander Rodchenko wearing the constructivist work overalls created by his wife Varvara Stepanova.
Photo Mikhail Kaufman, 1923.
Page from Bruce Bernard (ed.), Century: One Hundred Years of Human Progress, Regression, Suffering and Hope. London: Phaidon, 1999.

LEVI STRAUSS

Levi Strauss & Co. first patented its denim jeans, then known as waist overalls, in 1873. The trousers were made in San Francisco, where the company was based, with denim from the Amoskeag Mill in Manchester, New Hampshire. They had a single back pocket with Arcuate (interlocking double arc) stitching, a watch pocket, a cinch (half-belt), suspender buttons and a rivet in the crotch. The pockets were also riveted, a patented feature exclusive to Levi's. The origin of the arched stitching design is lost in time. In 1890 Levi's copper-riveted overalls were first given the '501' designation by which they would become famous.

These overalls stood the test of time, coming through the Great Depression and the Second World War, picking up minor modifications along the way: the single back pocket became a pair, the cinch was removed, the suspender buttons were replaced by belt loops. During the war, all superfluous detailing and decoration were removed in order to save materials, including the arched stitching design – so the machinists painted the familiar arched logo by hand onto the back pockets of every pair of jeans.

For reasons that remain unknown, teenagers began calling the product 'jeans' in the 1950s and this became the term used by all denim manufacturers. These five-pocket (two rear, two front and a ticket pocket) casual trousers became the uniform of youth over the next few decades. Originally all Levi's 501s were 'shrink to fit', and teenagers would take to the bathtub wearing their newly bought jeans in order to shrink them to their desired fit. In the early 1960s pre-shrunk jeans were introduced.

The Levi's red tab, with the word 'Levi's' stitched across it in white, first appeared in 1936 as a label to differentiate the jeans from others on the

Below **Levi's red tab details.**

Below right **Denim indigo dye vat.**

RESEARCH AND INSPIRATION 117

Above **Detail of farmer's blue jeans, boots and spurs. This man was once a cowboy and continued to dress as such afterwards. Pie Town, New Mexico, June 1940.**

Above right **Two gold miners standing outside the Last Chance Mine, wearing Levi's jeans. Placer County, California, c. 1882.**

market. The upper-case 'E' changed to a lower-case 'e' in 1971, and the 'Big E' became the identifying feature of vintage pieces, both jeans and jackets. In the mid-1980s vintage clothing started to gain mass appeal; Levi's Japan was the first branch of the company to start looking back in time with a view to reissuing vintage styles. In 1992 Levi's began to capitalize on its strong design heritage, introducing a high-end range called Capital E.

In 1993 Levi's initiated its 'Send Them Home Search', a competition to find the oldest pair of Levi's jeans in the United States, cleverly encouraging a whole nation to tap into the brand's longevity and heritage. The oldest pair submitted dated from the late 1920s. In 1996, building on the success of the Capital E range, a new series of vintage reproductions, called the Levi's Vintage Clothing line, was rolled out in stores worldwide.

In 1997 the company purchased a pair of 501 jeans dating from 1891 for $25,000 – vintage really was big business. The following year it celebrated the 125th anniversary of its blue jeans.

Levi's produces many styles, both new and reissued, but always tapping into the company's rich heritage to produce an unmistakably Levi's product.

LEE

Above **Lee denim work jacket, 1940s.**

Below **Lee Riders metal button and Storm Rider labels.**

Opposite **Lee Riders bandana.**

H. D. Lee started out in 1889 as a wholesale grocer, but by 1911 his company had branched out to become a workwear manufacturer, its first product being the Lee Bib Overall. These overalls were made of denim and had a multifunctional breast pocket and a button fly.

In 1913 Lee developed a coverall – a one-piece combination of jacket and dungarees known as the Lee Union-All. This product became the US Army's official fatigue uniform during the First World War. Lee's first jacket, designed in 1922 specifically for railroad workers, was named the Loco Jacket and set the template for the four-pocket American work jacket.

By the mid-1920s Lee had recognized the demand for Western wear for cowboys and horse riders, and was producing Lee Cowboy Pants, known as 101 jeans. In 1944 Lee put all its cowboy garments into the Riders range, including the 101 jeans (now featuring the 'Lazy S' stitching reminiscent of

longhorn cattle on the back pockets) and the now popular 101 jacket and its winter counterpart, the Storm Rider (see pp. 184–85).

The 1950s saw denim move from being just workwear to become the leisure wear of choice for the youth of the day. Rebel icons Marlon Brando and James Dean both starred in movies in this decade wearing jeans. By the 1970s Lee's focus was principally on the fashion market as opposed to workwear, although, that said, Lee remains the denim brand of choice for cowboys even now. The company continues to introduce new products to the fashion market, many of them referencing their best-selling vintage pieces such as the Storm Rider jacket and the 101 cowboy jeans.

CARHARTT WIP
(WORK IN PROGRESS)

'Carhartt goods are not cheap from the dollars and cents point of view, but when wear, service and satisfaction are taken into consideration, they are indeed the best value in the world.'

Hamilton Carhartt

Carhartt is one of the world's leading brands with a discernible crossover from workwear to street fashion today. The brand was founded by Hamilton Carhartt in Michigan in 1889, with the motto 'From the mill to millions'. It expanded during the early part of the twentieth century, with twenty factories and mills in North America and Europe.

Today its lifestyle division has stores in locations all over the world. In keeping with its heritage, many of the garments are still constructed with triple-stitched and copper-riveted seams and the denim and cotton duck fabrics that have become symbolic of the brand.

Carhartt's first garment as a manufacturer was an overall for railway workers, made in both denim and hard-wearing cotton canvas, also known as duck canvas (from the Dutch *doek*), and featuring the trademark ruler pocket and hammer loop.

Today, Carhartt has retained its status as America's premier workwear brand, but the appeal of its functional, long-lasting and classic garments has spread beyond tradespeople, and these pieces are now favoured by the trendy young.

In 1994, to reflect this, Work In Progress was founded and set up a distribution network for Carhartt across Europe, bringing a selection of classic products from the original workwear range into a new market. Carefully adapting and reinterpreting the classic designs and cuts, the brand enjoyed immediate success. Authentic Carhartt products became popular both with those aficionados of traditional American heritage garments as well as with musicians, skaters, BMX cyclists and artists.

Below **Carhartt WIP/APC collaboration jacket.**

Below right **A group of American hunters c. 1950.**

Opposite **Classic Carhartt work jacket.**

CONTEMPORARY WORKWEAR

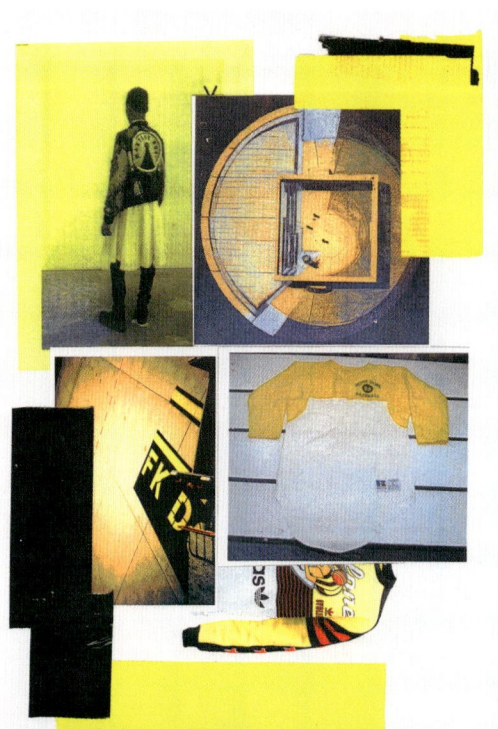

RESEARCH AND INSPIRATION

Workwear, as we know it today, is very much an American invention. Dickies is the world's largest maker of workwear and a popular youth brand, notably among the skateboarding fraternity.

Opposite, clockwise from left **Dickies Hi Vis vest; workwear-inspired research by Aaron Tubb, University of Westminster, London; workwear exhibition at Parsons The New School for Design, New York.**

Clockwise from top left **Research by Aaron Tubb; Dickies Hi Vis protective workwear; Dickies Hi Vis vest.**

CONTEMPORARY DENIM

The contemporary denim scene is thriving internationally, with San Francisco in the United States and Okayama in Japan establishing themselves as key design locations within the industry, and Amsterdam taking its place as the denim capital of Europe.

According to Amy Leverton, senior denim editor at Stylesight, 'The Amsterdam denim scene is key right now. Although many big players have been based here for a long time, such as G-Star and Scotch & Soda, newer names on the scene such as KOI (Kings of Indigo), Butcher of Blue and the more established Denham have been making waves.'

Central to the Amsterdam denim scene is the newly created House of Denim Jean School based at the ROC (Regional Community College) of Amsterdam. For students, the school provides a specifically denim-focused fashion education, and it is already proving to have an important role in uniting several notable names from the denim world through their involvement with the course. The Amsterdam Fashion Institute (AMFI) runs a six-month denim programme for third-year BA fashion design students that is designed to provide in-depth knowledge of all things denim.

Elsewhere, brands such as Raleigh, Tellason, Jack/Knife and Railcar Fine Goods in the United States, Iron Heart, Sugar Cane and the Flat Head in Japan, and Dawson Denim in the United Kingdom are taking a more artisanal approach to their businesses, turning to local manufacturers and utilizing vintage looms and machinery. As Leverton says, 'It's a movement that sees denim production move back to the smaller-scale businesses and celebrate true craftsmanship once again.'

Right **Timothy Everest Bespoke Casual denim jacket.**

Opposite **Details of Nigel Cabourn's denim collection; and a selvedge denim loom.**

THE LANGUAGE OF CLOTHES

All garment types have a specific DNA, set codes that define their manufacture and functionality. Once a designer totally understands these codes, this vocabulary, it gives design work an authenticity and integrity, as well as an opportunity to subvert successfully these codes in a thoughtful and knowing way.

One needs to question what it is that makes the language of tailoring differ from that of workwear, say, or sportswear. Look at the construction – is it lined, fused, single or double fabric? Is there topstitching, and is it single row, double, even triple? Which way is the seam pressed for that topstitching – open or to one side? Are the seams constructed for function – for strength, structure or waterproofing, perhaps? How are the different fabrics handled – denim as opposed to shirting or suiting? A garment type can also be defined by different detailing, such as the pockets or the collar shape. Again, once the designer has cracked these codes and has a firm understanding of the conventions, there is an opportunity to play with them and create something new and unique.

Different designers and manufacturers have, over the years, also developed their own languages, sometimes first for function, but also definitely for recognition: consider the Arcuate stitching on the back pockets of a pair of Levi's, the triple-stitched seams on a Carhartt jacket, or, more recently, the stitched-through label of a Margiela sweater. One ought to learn the subtle nuances of menswear's cuts and finishes, and to be able to differentiate between Savile Row, Japanese and Italian tailoring.

Such seemingly mundane questions and observations are at the heart of what I call the language of clothes and are fundamental to fashion design in general, and to menswear in particular, the latter being based, as it is, on a series of strict codes. Menswear design requires this level of knowledge, and perhaps even obsession, to make it believable and successful.

Below **British Naval Intelligence agent Captain George B. Osborne, wearing a yachting cap and striped jersey, 1948.**

Below right **Nautical-inspired mood board by Charlotte Scott, University of Westminster, London.**

Opposite left **Junya Watanabe Breton stripes and oilskin jacket, Spring/Summer 2011.**

Opposite right **Dior Breton-style sweater, Spring/Summer 2013.**

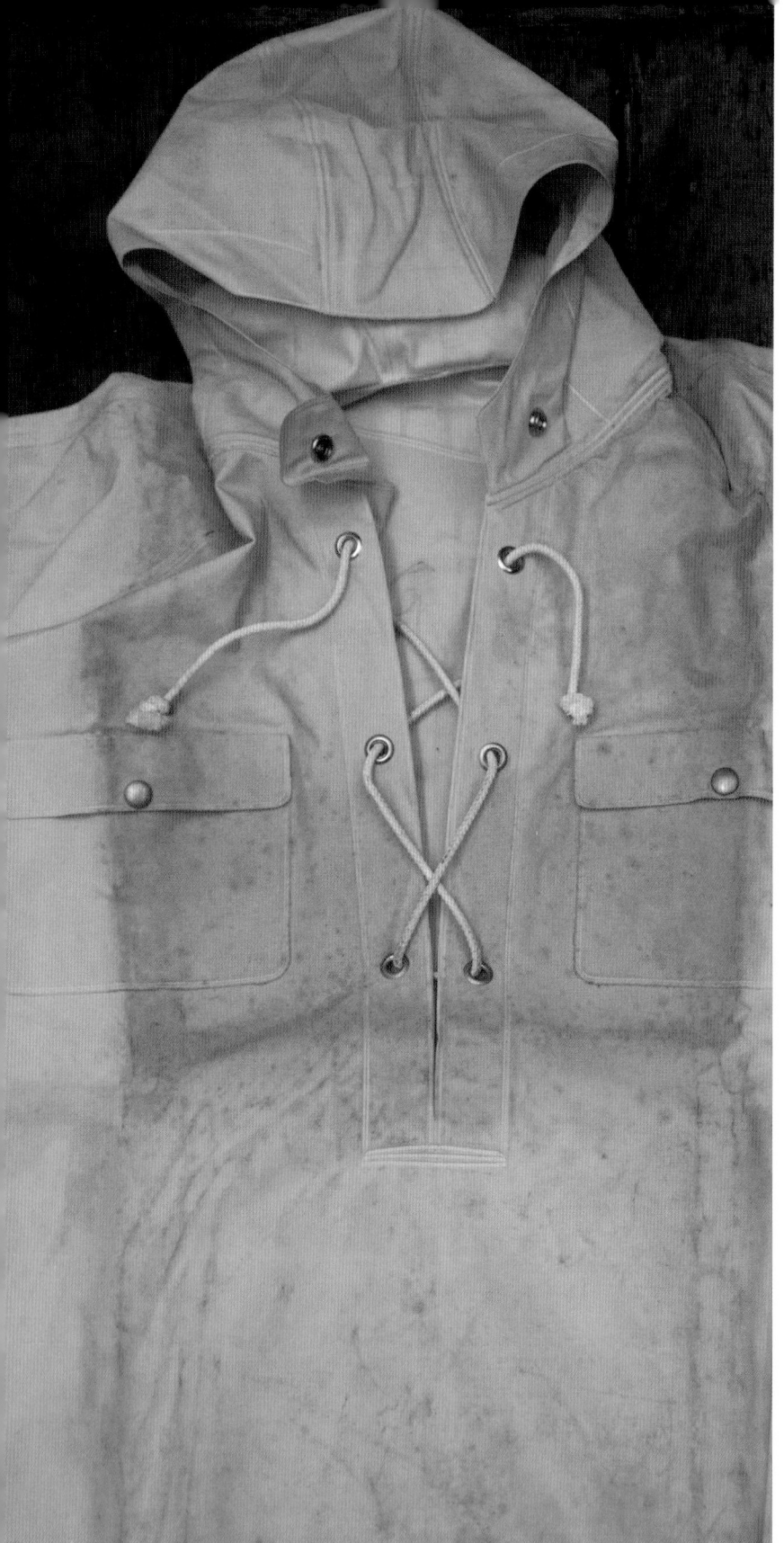

GARMENT CASE STUDY
OILSKINS

Left Vintage oilskin jacket at The Vintage Showroom.

Opposite, clockwise from top Fishermen in oilskins, Alaska, January 1990; Thom Browne-designed Moncler nautical collection, Spring/Summer 2013; vintage postcard of fisherman in sou'wester.

KNIT CASE STUDY
FAIR ISLE

Fair Isle is the most remote inhabited island in the United Kingdom and is famous for its traditional knitting. The term 'Fair Isle' is now often used generically for coloured knitting with horizontal bands of differing geometric patterns, but this unique style developed on Fair Isle centuries ago, when local knitters discovered that fine yarns stranded into a double layer produce durable, warm, lightweight garments. ('Stranded colour-work' is the more accurate term for the generic technique.)

Traditional Fair Isle patterns, worked in the round, usually have a limited palette of five or so colours and use two colours per row. Knitwear featuring original patterns worked in the traditional colours of red, blue, brown, yellow and white was historically much sought after for its unique value, but during the 1920s Fair Isle sweaters knitted in natural wool colours (brown, grey, fawn and white) became highly fashionable after the Prince of Wales (later King Edward VIII) wore a Fair Isle tank top, knitted by Maggie Bruce and given to him during his visit to the island in 1921 (see p. 58).

Today the only source of the genuine article remains Fair Isle, where a small co-operative – Fair Isle Crafts – produces traditional and contemporary sweaters on hand-frame machines, quality-controlled and labelled with Fair Isle's own trademark.

Maverick London knit trio Sibling (see pp. 26–27) often employ the techniques of Fair Isle but bring their own unique aesthetic to the age-old methods. Cozette McCreery of Sibling says: 'Many of our designs are strongly rooted in what are pretty traditional forms, patterns and ideas, Fair Isles being one of them. Our most influential and imitated form of Fair Isle we renamed Scare Isle. Knitted in a cashmere–wool blend in eye-dazzling neons, the traditional pattern is punctuated with a skull and a Frankenstein portrait based on sketches by artist Will Broome. Knitted into a turtleneck, leggings and gilet, the outfit was made more monstrous as topped off with a raffia Mohawk balaclava. Knit Monster ... now travels the world as part of "Wool Modern" as well as gaining book covers and more press than all three of us put together.'

Below Illustration from a vintage knitting pattern.

Below centre Advertisement for distinctive golf hose, 1920s.

Below right Catalogue illustration of a Fair Isle sweater, 1920s.

Opposite Sibling's George and the Dragon Fair Isle sweater.

Overleaf left Walter Van Beirendonck Fair Isle sweater from the Autumn/Winter 2010 'Take a W-Ride' collection.

Overleaf right Nigel Cabourn Fair Isle sweaters.

RESEARCH AND INSPIRATION   133

Crew Neck Fairisle Jumper 100% British Wool

BRITISH ISLES Lettering?
double rib?
single rib?

— thistle
— daffodil
— double rib

sunflower

big
thistle +
daffodil

small
shamrock
+ roses.

Colours:
pale Aqua — background
mustard/gold — daffodil
green/blue donegal — Leaves + shamrock
pale pink — rose
rust? — thistle

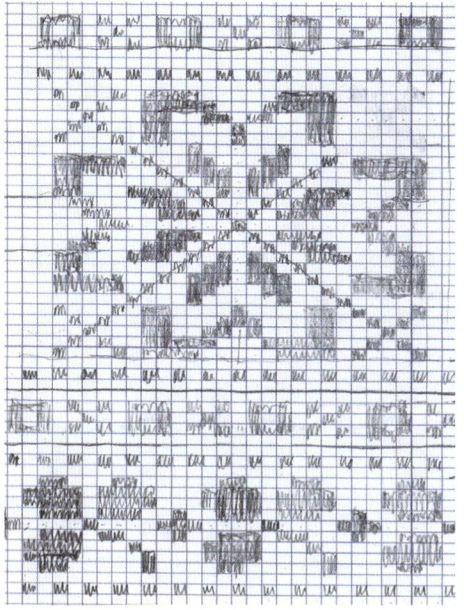

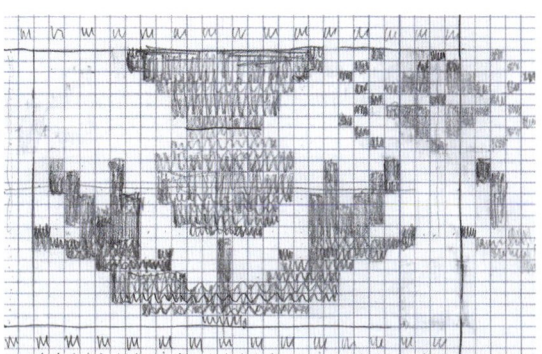

RESEARCH AND INSPIRATION

knit slipover

traditional / Fair Isle pattern

Flower pattern / Fair Isle.

Fair Isle-inspired sketchbook pages by Amelia Peters, Central Saint Martins, London.

SPORTSWEAR

The earliest sportswear was designed with recognition in mind, the colours, colour blocking, stripes and insignia all there to aid in the identification of a particular team or side. Fabrics were basic in the days before stretchy or water-resistant fabrics, so sports garments were made from cottons and wools – hardly what we would call 'performance' fabrics these days.

Initially teams and colleges came up with their own logos, but gradually sportswear manufacturers devised logos for themselves too, and these were often seen on garments alongside team logos and crests. Notable examples include the Jantzen Diving Girl of the 1920s, the Lacoste crocodile of the 1930s, the Adidas three stripes (an unusual case of a non-graphic logo that has been trademarked successfully) and the Nike 'swoosh', which was designed in 1971 by Portland State University graphics student Carolyn Davidson.

As fabric and manufacturing technologies improved, a whole new breed of materials and techniques arose, including man-made fibres, stretch fabrics and fabrics with performance-enhancing properties. Machines that overlocked and flatlocked seams enabled garments to stretch and move as never before, and to be non-chafing.

These technologies and fabrics have also informed developments in fashion. All designers seek the new, and often it is these developments in sportswear that inspire them.

Below **Two men in cricket whites**, *c.* 1870.

Below right **Vintage advertisement featuring Edwardian sporting colours.**

Opposite top **Hockey team**, *c.* 1950.

Opposite bottom **Rugby fifteen**, 1920s.

BASEBALL AND LETTERMAN JACKETS

Above **Vintage baseball jacket.**

Opposite, clockwise from top left **Vintage letterman sweater label; James Otis 'Doc' Crandall, St Louis Terriers (Federal League) baseball player, wearing a sweater with 'St. L' emblem, 1914; 1960s American short-sleeved jacket; photograph of a man in a letterman sweater, c. 1920; American high-school baseball team, c. 1970.**

As with most menswear staples, the classic American baseball jacket has a long history. It was originally known as a letterman jacket or an award jacket, and was worn by members of student teams at university or college (hence its alternative name, the varsity jacket).

The wearing of team colours dates back to mid-Victorian times, and by the end of the nineteenth century sweaters were worn in team colours and bearing names and logos. Often given as prizes, these sweaters began to be called award sweaters.

The beginning of the twentieth century saw the arrival of the letterman jacket, with its leather sleeves and wool body. By the 1930s letters started to appear on these jackets, as they had on the sweaters.

In the 1950s an American company, Phoenix Lettering, began embroidering chenille motifs on these sweaters and jackets; this is the raised lettering that is found on letterman jackets to this day.

Traditionally, the team member's name was sewn on the left pocket, the year of graduation on the right pocket, and the sport played on the right sleeve. To show loyalty to one's team the varsity letter was sewn on to the left chest, over the heart.

These jackets have evolved to become what today are popularly known as baseball or varsity jackets. While primarily commercial products, promoting the name of a company or team, they closely follow the traditional formula of leather sleeves, wool body and insignia that was established by the originals.

RESEARCH AND INSPIRATION 139

CONCEPT-LED AND AVANT-GARDE

Although menswear is very much about product and well-defined parameters, every discipline still needs visionaries to push it forward, to take risks, to rethink and reinvent the genre. We need designers with true vision, conviction and even a sense of humour.

The ideas should never be more important than the final outcome (the clothes), but the design process can differ from what is considered the norm.

Walter Van Beirendonck, Spring/Summer 2009 show finale.

The following pages present the work of concept-led designers, all very different in their approach; some are professionals and some are students on journeys to becoming professionals. We see Belgian designer Walter Van Beirendonck with his quirky future-fashion and cartoon-like aesthetics, German-born Bernhard Willhelm with his pop references from toys, computer games and American football, and Britain's conceptualist Aitor Throup, who shuns the seasonal merry-go-round for a more cerebral approach to the whole process. Japanese designer Junya Watanabe often takes a particular garment type then reinvents it over and over, while streetwear brand XXBC is inspired by the quirky individuality of New York street fashion.

According to Andrew Groves, course director at the University of Westminster, London, 'while a lot of contemporary menswear is about revisiting and adapting the essential "codes" of menswear such as tailoring, Savile Row, sportswear and uniform, it is also vital that there are designers that are iconoclastic in their approach and conceptual in their output. Designers such as Thom Browne or Walter Van Beirendonck push menswear into areas where it has previously not dared venture by looking at either cyber technology or gender, identity and sexuality in ways that are both exciting and provocative. These designers push the boundaries further, and ultimately enable other designers to move the parameters of their work and menswear in general forward.'

On pushing creativity within the field, Stephanie Cooper, menswear lecturer at Central Saint Martins, says: 'Without those designers who loosen the screws of the machine to create challenge and impact, and who rebel and explore limits of wearability, that are the purest manifestations of a designer's ideas, the advancement of design concepts and fabric technology would be unable to find a language to move out of the restrictions of tradition.

'Historical fashion is considered and then re-created until it has radically evolved towards an intuitive and reactive solution, creating a transformation of the aesthetics of the time. The vocabulary of conceptual clothing is a way of addressing identity, the body and gender. These designs are sometimes not intended for production but serve as an abundant source of innovation, unaffected by commerciality, that exists as a purely aesthetic representation of fashion as an aspiration, a dream or an art form.'

As to where menswear designers might look for new and fresh inspirations, Sharon Graubard of Stylesight cites womenswear as one potential source. 'I think menswear can look more at womenswear,' she says, 'and some menswear designers are already doing that. J. W. Anderson comes to mind, with his Autumn/Winter 2013 collection: it had flounces and gathers. Steven Cox and Daniel Silver of Duckie Brown in New York draw from womenswear as well, but in a subtle way.'

JUNYA WATANABE

Born in 1961, Japanese designer Junya Watanabe was a protégé of Rei Kawakubo, joining Comme des Garçons as a pattern cutter in 1984 after graduating from Tokyo's Bunka Fashion College. He went on to design the Comme des Garçons womenswear line Robe de Chambre (now discontinued). Since 2001 he has worked on his own Junya Watanabe Man label within the Comme des Garçons range.

Watanabe has a particular talent for reworking and reinvention, often taking a single garment type or genre as the core piece or theme for a collection and deconstructing the elements – reworking them into something new and wonderful, but always with the source remaining completely recognizable. To this end he has collaborated with numerous manufacturers of archetypal garments and products. Levi's denim, Carhartt workwear and Vanson's leathers have all been transformed by the Watanabe magic, as have the shoes of Converse, Puma and Trickers, all top brands in their respective field. Recent collaborations have included Loewe luxury leather goods and Lyle & Scott knitwear.

There is probably no better designer alive who can take the DNA of a brand or the language of an archetypal, even ubiquitous, piece of clothing, and reinvent it while staying absolutely true to the original code of the design.

Watanabe's menswear often has elements that are reversible or detachable, maybe implying that a garment is not a finite solution: what these features do allow for is input from the wearer, who then plays a part in the design process.

Watanabe is a designer who has mostly eschewed the design language of his native Japan in order to reinterpret and repackage the West, before selling it back stamped with his own remarkable design skills.

Right Junya Watanabe workwear-inspired collection, Autumn/Winter 2012, Paris.

Opposite Junya Watanabe, Autumn/Winter 2009, Paris.

AITOR THROUP

'I have drawn for as long as I can remember, and clothing became a natural platform through which I could develop all the ideas that had so far been limited to the two-dimensional constraints of pencil and paper.'

Born in Buenos Aires, Argentina, in 1980, Aitor Throup moved to Burnley, Lancashire, in 1992, where he grew up and developed a passion for labels such as Stone Island and C. P. Company. Throup's interest in these brands coupled with his talent for drawing led him to take a BA course in Fashion Design at Manchester Metropolitan University. In 2006 he completed an MA in Fashion Menswear at the Royal College of Art in London.

In January 2013 the conceptual designer and artist revealed his first full ready-to-wear range, part of his ongoing 'New Object Research' project. Six years in the making, the presentation consisted of multiple suspended life-size human sculptures, each wearing a different iteration of one of four complete outfits; together they made up a twenty-piece collection.

The presentation featured a live soundscape by Sergio Pizzorno of rock band Kasabian (Throup is currently the band's creative director) who performed an exclusive sonic composition inspired by Throup's various research themes, which included everything from the Hindu religion to the culture, people and costumes of Mongolia.

So far in his career Throup has continuously challenged the cyclical structure of the fashion industry. He has avoided the launch of a commercially available line in favour of creating a unique business model that allows him to showcase his product innovation periodically, while being able to work on new concepts without the fashion business's predetermined time constraints and seasonal pressures.

In October 2012 the Aitor Throup studio released four archetypes (a jacket, a T-shirt, trousers and a backpack) exclusively available through Rei Kawakubo's Dover Street Market in London as part of its Open House event and coinciding with London's Frieze Art Fair. February 2013 saw the launch of Throup's first commercially available product, the Shiva Skull Bag.

On the subject of his own design work, Throup says: 'I consider my approach to be that of a product designer, rather than a fashion designer, so every piece for me has an archetypal element of its own within the context of its original concept and/or narrative.'

Aitor Throup's 'New Object Research' presentation, January 2013.

CASE STUDY
LIAM HODGES, ROYAL COLLEGE OF ART, LONDON

Liam Hodges of the Royal College of Art, London, took inspiration from Morris dancers for his BA graduate collection. His research materials and sketches are shown here.

'The research book for me is a starting point in all my projects/collections. I use photocopying and printouts, pages kept from magazines and pulled off my bedroom wall. It's a way for me to realize my aesthetic and pull together all of my inspiration in one place. The process of formatting pushes me again to look at the images and decide, if they are relevant, why they are relevant. It's always good to help me reassess and justify previous decisions.

'In this case I was looking at Morris dancers but I needed a way to show who my Morris man is – why he isn't like the ordinary one. I used music references from punk, hardcore metal and hip-hop to the utilitarian military images of combatant gear, as well as Wiccan references to the straw bear and pagan images of the savage.'

XXBC

Streetwear label XXBC ('twenty BC') reflects the individuality, eclecticism and occasional eccentricity of the characters on the streets of New York. The brand was created by Alex Lee and Will Thompson, self-proclaimed lovers of the hip-hop and street cultures of the 1980s and 1990s. They take individually sourced vintage fabrics, mix them up with more traditional sportswear fabrics and have them carefully manufactured to give each garment the quality, individuality and exclusivity that they both feel is missing from much of today's mass-produced sportswear.

Their own eclecticism is very much apparent in both their garments and the way they present themselves to the world. Lee is a keen street-style photographer and blogger, and it is evident that the individuality and diversity he documents on the streets in his photographic work feeds back into the duo's designs.

Lee says: 'We got together with the notion that we could merge art and history through clothing. And to use history to make something contemporary that will, in turn, influence the future. Okay, that sounds like a lot, but at the end of the day we're just two young guns who like to make cool clothing.'

Right **Portrait of Will Thompson and Alex Lee.**

Opposite **XXBC's sweatshirts made from 'found' vintage fabrics and more traditional sportswear fabrics.**

**CASE STUDY
MARIOS ALEXANDROU,
KINGSTON UNIVERSITY,
LONDON**

'The theme of my final collection was "Mines", with the concept of "Trails of Destruction".

'The starting point for this project was an old and neglected landmark in my home town back in Cyprus. This mine is full of rusted objects and the ecosystem around it has been affected. These signs of a destroyed location motivated and inspired me to tell the story through my designs.

'My development reflects the theme through the contour lines that represent the topographical changes of the ground. The rich colours and textures hugely influenced my ideas as I used fabrics and textile quilting that has these effects.

'The key inspiration behind my collection was in fact the red lake that sits in the centre of the mine. It formed from the rain and because of the copper and rust in the surrounding ground turned red.

'This mine is important to me not only because it is a part of my village and my childhood memories but also because my grandfather worked there for many years. His stories inspired me to transform these landmark memories into a story of clothes.

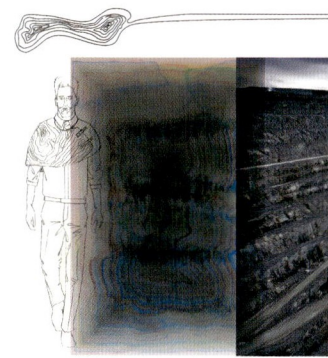

'These mine tailings surround the village, "decorating" the hills. Rusty, lonely, forgotten and frozen in place and time, these "creatures" now coexist with trees, plants and the rest of nature. They have inevitably become part of the landscape and been embraced by nature.

'Therefore the concept was formed around the idea of forgotten and neglected objects and people. This lonely wanderer harmoniously coexisting with forgotten landscapes.

'Artists Yayoi Kusama, Chen Jiagang and Christine Beau influenced the design development process. Kusama's *Flowers Overcoat* (1964) inspired me to think of clothes as part of nature. As a result I started developing my own techniques of fabric manipulation or embellishments. Chen's photography influenced my concept as he uses similar locations to express feelings of neglect and ignorance. Finally Christine Beau's paintings led me to develop my quilting using linear designs.

'The influences above formed the body of research that helped me develop my capsule menswear collection.

'The aim of this project was to produce a modern and fresh collection that drew on staples of traditional men's clothing like soft and luxurious wools and classic menswear shapes.

'I referenced contemporary menswear designers whose work I admire and look up to. Kim Jones and his successful path inspired me to design

Marios Alexandrou of Kingston University, London, took inspiration from a mine near his home town for his BA graduate collection. His research materials are shown here.

with luxurious textures and interesting materials. Martin Margiela and Raf Simons are also influential figures when I design.

'To sum up, the journey of designing my graduate collection took a very interesting path and its narrative features took me as a designer on my own personal journey of memories and visuals.

'The collection has soft and luxurious textures, pale and harmonious colours, but some accent rusty reds and dark aubergines, as well as camel beige, to express the warmth and golden colours of the mine in Mitsero, Cyprus.'

**CASE STUDY
JAMES PAWSON,
UNIVERSITY OF
WESTMINSTER,
LONDON**

'I look towards fields beyond fashion, not simply to source inspiration but to broaden my ideas and perception of fashion. I try to see clothing as a product that has been engineered and constructed, to see how one element can inform the next, resulting in a functioning piece of design. From investigating three-dimensional designs, I experiment with translating the construction and finishings within product design and architecture and applying it to the body, and in doing so challenge the norms of fashion. Drawing from a love of modern, simple and functional design, I create fashion that is not simply beautiful but purposeful, and design modern menswear that is beautiful because of its functionality, rather than restricting it. The simple yet considered nature of my work has developed from both my independent work as a designer and my experience and work within the industry. Working in environments where quality and execution have been foremost, I have learned the skill and the importance of presentation and the beauty of finish, understanding how tradition and execution are key when creating modern, innovative clothing. My work has become an extension of myself and distinctive to me. My aesthetic is a result of my research and sourcing beyond fashion.'

James Pawson of the University of Westminster, London, looked beyond fashion for the inspiration behind his BA graduate collection. His research materials and collection are shown here.

BERNHARD WILLHELM

Born in Germany in 1972, Bernhard Willhelm studied at the Royal Academy of Fine Arts in Antwerp, Belgium. After graduating he worked for Walter Van Beirendonck in Antwerp as well as Vivienne Westwood in London.

Willhelm describes himself as a postmodern designer and is obsessed by pop culture: McDonald's Happy Meal figures, dinosaurs, computer games and American footballers are all cited as his inspirations. He launched his menswear line in 2000 and first showed in Paris three years later. With their sportswear feel, his clothes perhaps defy the conventions of traditional menswear. They might have recognizable graphic elements, or those of folk costume from his native Bavaria as well as African cultures, but they also veer towards the deliberately absurd.

In an interview with *Hint* magazine in 2005, Willhelm said: 'I see myself as part of a generation. I really appreciate what others are about, people like Raf Simons, Wendy & Jim, Haider Ackermann. And I used to like Viktor & Rolf. Haider and I were in the same class.'

Of his design process he went on to say: 'When I'm designing, I don't see the clothes as crazy. I've got to exaggerate to find the essence of an idea. In starting a collection, the most important thing is to bring an idea out quite clearly. Fashion people only react to very strong ideas. One season I was into rubbish, so I based the collection on McDonald's Happy Meal figures. That's all I needed. I design to express something. Cutting myself off completely, then being free to do whatever I want has always appealed to me. I always had the feeling I was in a prison. Maybe that's why I've always chased the exotic.'

Bernhard Willhelm,
Autumn/Winter 2012.

WALTER VAN BEIRENDONCK

Walter Van Beirendonck was born in Belgium in 1957 and graduated from the Royal Academy of Fine Arts in Antwerp in 1980, the same year as Dirk Van Saene, Dries Van Noten and Ann Demeulemeester. Marina Yee graduated the following year and Dirk Bikkembergs a year later. Collectively these designers became known as the Antwerp Six. Van Beirendonck began producing his own collections in 1983.

His collections always have a strong theme or identity, which he sources from various elements of inspiration. 'I'm permanently researching and looking for new ideas,' he says: 'rituals, art, ethnic tribes, music, history and historic garments... The world around me is my inspiration. I'm collecting images and everything I find I like I put in scrapbooks and photobooks.

'And at a certain moment, when the direction is clear for me, I start to sketch the complete looks, as they will be presented on the catwalk. I decide styling, hair and make-up, together with the garments, colours and fabrics.'

All of this results in what he calls 'a very recognizable Walter-signature' – a mix of cartoon-like sportswear and what appears at first to be classic tailoring but on closer inspection has an extraordinary complexity of cut and manufacture, all topped off with often outrageous styling to evoke the particular message of each individual collection.

Van Beirendonck is interested in the ways in which new and modern technology can be applied to fashion. 'I do like technology,' he says, 'and I have done and still do a lot of experiments with fabrics and techniques coming out of fields such as security, sport and safety. But, on the other hand, I'm really disappointed that the techniques for making clothes have hardly evolved since 1900 – it is still about cutting a fabric and stitching it together.

'I hope that the evolution in 3D printing will evolve into the direction of softer materials, giving us fashion designers the possibility to introduce this new technique into our collections, next to tailoring and traditional crafts.'

Van Beirendonck's work may be seen as very much 'future fashion', but in terms of inspiration the designer does not ignore menswear and historical men's clothing.

'I do like the future, but I also embrace the past,' he says. 'Actually, I think that for the last five seasons I've been working on a "Future-Dandy" direction. I do love to research the history of clothing, and the "Incroyable/Revolution" period is one of my favourite periods in men's garment history.' This was part of the aftermath of the French Revolution that saw a subculture of fashionable Parisian aristocrats dressing in luxury and decadence as a reaction to the Reign of Terror. 'My "Revolution" collection,' says Van Beirendonck, 'was a remake/rethinking of exactly that amazing moment in history.'

Opposite top and right **Walter Van Beirendonck's 'Lust Never Sleeps' collection, Autumn/Winter 2012.**

Opposite bottom **Portrait of Walter Van Beirendonck.**

RESEARCH AND INSPIRATION 157

3
GARMENT BIOGRAPHIES

The Trench Coat 160

The Pea Coat 164

Case Study:
Philip Strawbridge 170

The Parka 172

The Motorcycle Jacket 178

The Denim Jacket 182

The Flying Jacket 188

The Duffle Coat 194

The Field Jacket 200

THE TRENCH COAT

Above Four businessmen in trench coats line up for a photograph, c. 1940.

Opposite, clockwise from top left Thresher trench coat advertising from the time of the First World War; two photographs of First World War soldiers in trench coats; vintage trench coats; spec drawing of a trench coat by Aaron Tubb, University of Westminster, London.

Overleaf left Burberry Prorsum trench coat, Autumn/Winter 2010.

Overleaf right A Child of the Jago trench coat, Spring/Summer 2013.

The origins of the trench coat are imprecise, with both Burberry and Aquascutum claiming it as their own design. Certainly the first registered design was by Burberry in 1901, and it has since become the signature garment of both of these fashion houses.

The original trench coats, developed for the military, were made of weatherproof cloth and had D-rings and straps for the attachment of epaulettes and lanyards. The rings we still see on the belt today were originally intended to attach map holders and swords.

Used during the First World War and dubbed 'trench coat' by the front-line troops, the garment found favour in both menswear and womenswear after the war ended. Usually in black, khaki or beige waterproof cloth, it took its place in civilian life as a practical garment.

Typically double-breasted with raglan sleeves, epaulettes, a belt with D-rings, storm flaps and a deep rear vent with button closure, the trench coat has since become a symbol of cool, worn as it was by Humphrey Bogart's Rick Blaine character in the movie *Casablanca* (1942), by comic-strip hero Dick Tracy and slung over the arm of rumpled detective Columbo.

Very much a menswear staple today, the trench coat makes regular appearances in the collections of many of the world's leading menswear designers, including the more esoteric Japanese collections, and remains the subject of endless reworking by the Burberry design team to this day.

GARMENT BIOGRAPHIES 161

THE THRESHER
TRENCH COAT

Officially brought to the notice of OFFICERS COMMANDING CORPS of the British Expeditionary Force.

A coat that serves as a Rain-coat, Great Coat, British Warm, and when fitted with blanket lining (see page 28) an Emergency Sleeping Kit.

July 17th, 1916.

Your Trench Coat which I bought about a year ago continues to be satisfactory, and with the sheepskin lining is superior to the leather clothing issued to officers of the R.F.C.

Capt. ————
Seaforth Highlanders,
attd. R.F.C.

January 27th, 1917.

Enclose cheque ———. The Trench Coat has done well, and I think you have received a good many orders from this Force from officers who have asked my opinion on it.

Capt. ————
H.Q. 8th Brigade,
Mesopotamia E.F.

May 23rd, 1916.

Last night we had a tropical thunderstorm for over four hours, and your coat kept me quite dry.

Lt.-Col. ————
Manchester Regt.

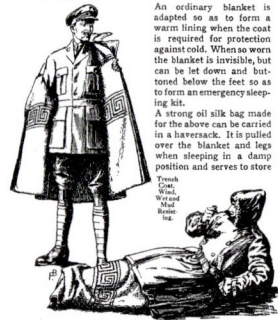

THE TRENCH and CAMPAIGN COAT
With detachable CAMEL HAIR BLANKET LINING.

An ordinary blanket is adapted so as to form a warm lining when the coat is required for protection against cold. When so worn the blanket is invisible, but can be let down and buttoned below the feet so as to form an emergency sleeping kit.

A strong oil silk bag made for the above can be carried in a haversack. It is pulled over the blanket and legs when sleeping in a damp position and serves to store

Trench
Coat,
Wind,
Wet and
Mud
Resisting.

As an Emergency Sleeping Kit.

the blanket when not in use as a coat lining. The advantage of a detachable hood makes the sleeping kit complete.

Coat and Blanket complete ... £6 16 6
Detachable Hood 0 12 6
Oil Silk Leg Bag, Reinforced Drill 0 17 6

THE PEA COAT

The Commander Overcoat

The Reefer Overcoat

Clockwise from top left Boys' pea coats from the early twentieth century; street-style shot; British Merchant Navy poster by Charles Wood, 1942; US Navy pea coats worn during the First World War.

Opposite US Navy pea coat.

UNIFORM REGULATIONS
UNITED STATES NAVY
NAVY DEPARTMENT
1913
(REVISED TO JANUARY 15, 1917)

Seaman   Chief Petty Officer

The life-line is firm
thanks to the
MERCHANT NAVY

This page Spec drawing of a pea coat by Aaron Tubb; vintage pea coats; pea-coat button with anchor motif.

Opposite, clockwise from top left US Navy pea coat label; vintage pea coat; European naval pea coat.

Overleaf Seamen in reefer jackets, c. 1900.

Overleaf right Balmain pea coat, Autumn/Winter 2011.

The pea coat is an overcoat of heavy dark navy-blue or black wool that was originally worn by the sailors of European navies. It has a high double-breasted front, broad rounded lapels, almost vertical slash or welt pockets at wrist level and a rear vent. A characteristic detail is its large buttons engraved with anchors or nautical insignia.

While the term 'pea jacket' first appeared in 1717, according to the Oxford English Dictionary, 'pea coat' did not arise for another hundred years or so. The name may have its origins in the Dutch word *pijjekker*, in which *pij* referred to a type of coarse, twilled blue cloth with a nap to the face side and *jekker* meant jacket. Others suggest that the name derives from 'pilot jacket', abbreviated to 'P jacket' (after the heavy coarse cloth from which it was made: pilot or P-cloth).

The coat was originally worn by crew members known as reefers, responsible for reducing the sails in a strong wind. Since it was worn when climbing, the jacket was cut short for ease of movement. Its double-breasted front, which displaces the buttons to each side, may have been designed to help reduce the chance of getting caught on the rigging, or alternatively, to provide a highly windproof fastening. Whatever the reason, it remains double-breasted to this day.

The coat was adopted by the US Navy in the early twentieth century from Britain's Royal Navy reefer jacket. At some point soon after the Second World War, the pea coat changed in design from an eight- to a six-button fastening, making for a longer and broader revers. Nowadays, in the United States, the reefer (worn by officers) is identical to the basic design but has gold insignia buttons and epaulettes; the bridge coat is the longer version.

The now classic pea coat has become a fashion staple, worn by servicemen and by the fashion-conscious worldwide; and is a perennial catwalk favourite for menswear designers and brands.

CASE STUDY
PHILIP STRAWBRIDGE, CENTRAL SAINT MARTINS, LONDON

THE PEA COAT

Philip Strawbridge of Central Saint Martins, London, researched the origins of the pea coat and the parka for his BA graduate collection. His mood boards and final collection are shown here.

THE DUFFLE PARKA

THE PARKA

The word 'parka' is derived from the Nenets language of northern Russia and simply means 'animal skin'. The garment known as the parka was a heavy, hooded jacket used by the Inuit of the Arctic.

From these Arctic origins, the parka was developed in the United States during the early 1950s for military flight crews stationed in extremely cold areas, and designed for temperatures as low as -50°C (-58°F). Made with a sage-green flight-silk outer and lining, the USAF N-3B parka was three-quarter length and had an attached hood. It was padded with a thick woollen fabric until the mid-1970s, when the padding became synthetic wadding and the outer shell was changed from silk to a man-made nylon fabric. The early parkas had real fur trims to their hoods, while later versions used synthetic fur. The hoods could be zipped right up for warmth, leaving only a small tunnel to look out of, leading these coats to be dubbed 'snorkel parkas'. Original manufacturers for the military included Alpha and Avirex, both of which still manufacture men's outerwear.

The N-3B parka design was appropriated for the civilian market by a variety of manufacturers, some of which remained faithful to the original specs, while others produced an inferior product. In Britain, the snorkel parka peaked in popularity in the early to mid-1980s when its inexpensive and hardy qualities made it popular among school children. School parkas usually had a quilted orange lining, unlike the original N-3B lining, which was un-quilted and sage green like the shell.

As one former schoolchild of the 1980s put it: 'There is a significant number of men from my generation who managed to get through school with the snorkel fully zipped up – safe in their own little comfort zone, seeing the world through a rabbit-fur-lined lens.'

The snorkel parka went on to become associated with geeks, nerds and trainspotters and its popularity faded in the late 1980s. A decade later, however, it became associated with the indie music scene, being worn by the likes of Liam Gallagher and the Pet Shop Boys – immortalized in the now iconic image by Eric Watson. By the 2000s the parka was a mainstream fashion garment once more.

The fishtail parka has a slightly different set of associations, being designed for use during the Korean War, with a longer, curved, split back (hence the name 'fishtail'), a feature that enabled the parka to be tied around the upper legs for added protection from the elements.

During the 1960s in the United Kingdom, the fishtail parka became the favoured outerwear of the mods. Widely available from army surplus shops, the parka was seen as the ideal garment for protecting their sharp suits worn beneath from dirt or oil kicked up by their scooters.

Spec drawings of a parka by Aaron Tubb, University of Westminster, London.

GARMENT BIOGRAPHIES 173

Left Parka-inspired jacket by Junya Watanabe, Autumn/Winter 2006.

Below Thomas Gushue, mate on Robert Peary's 1908–9 North Pole expedition, wearing a fur parka, Battle Harbor, Labrador.

Above Jack Tchernawitz, a Russian-born US Army major, wearing his parka at a delivery point of American supplies to Russia, somewhere in Iran, 1943.

Right Cut-outs from the sketchbook of Christopher Pak, University of Westminster, London.

GARMENT BIOGRAPHIES 175

Left A group of mods with their scooters in Brighton for a bank holiday, c. 1964.

This page Three views of a vintage parka.

Overleaf Vintage fishtail parka with lining visible in the centre image.

THE MOTORCYCLE JACKET

Motorcycle jackets were first seen in the early twentieth century, though the jackets used for motorcycle riding in the 1920s and 1930s were more akin to aviator or military-style jackets with button fronts and stand collars. Also seen were button-fronted coats constructed from thick horsehide, used extensively by both the military for flying jackets and the civilian population for workwear.

Harley-Davidson, which set up its motorcycle business in 1906, was an early manufacturer of quality leather jackets, and by the 1940s its Cycle Champ for men and Cycle Queen for women were considered the epitome of style. Other manufacturers such as Langlitz Leathers and Lewis Leathers also incorporated the D-shaped pocket of the Harley-Davidson jackets.

Schott NYC was founded by the brothers Irving and Jack Schott in 1913 and in 1928 produced the first ever leather motorcycle jacket. Retailing for $5.50, the Perfecto jacket achieved cult status when Marlon Brando wore it in the movie *The Wild One* (1953), in which a motorcycle gang terrorizes a small town. Its popularity increased even further when it was worn regularly by movie star James Dean. Seen as the garment of choice for the rebel, leather jackets were subsequently banned by school systems across the United States, thereby sealing their popularity among rebellious youth.

The leather biker jacket never lost its sense of cool and was later adopted by the punk movement in the late 1970s.

Langlitz Leathers is another great manufacturer of leather jackets that are known worldwide for their quality. Founded in 1947 in Portland, Oregon, it offers a bespoke service. The British Lewis Leathers, established in 1892, produces a wide range of leather jackets favoured by aficionados, particularly the Japanese; Japan is always a strong market for well-made classic garments. Vanson of Fall River, Massachusetts, founded in 1974, has a reputation for the finest-quality jackets; it has collaborated with Japanese designer Junya Watanabe on a couple of occasions, combining cutting-edge design with traditional styling and the best of leather manufacturing.

Below **Junya Watanabe** leather jacket produced in collaboration with Vanson, Autumn/Winter 2007.

Below right **Two vintage** leather jackets.

Opposite **Schott Perfecto** leather jacket.

Above **Motorcycle enthusiasts find a space for their prized possessions outside the Ace Café, a well-known meeting spot for bikers in 1960s London.**

Right **Motorcycle cops outside Langlitz Leathers, Portland, Oregon, c. 1960.**

Opposite **Film still from *The Wild One* (1953): Johnny Strabler (Marlon Brando) and his gang stand together on the pavement.**

THE DENIM JACKET

This page **Type 2 1950s Levi's jacket.**

Opposite **RRL pleated-front denim jacket, Autumn/Winter 2003.**

Above **A cowboy sharpens his knife, wearing an unknown brand of pleated-front denim jacket. Round-up near Marfa, Texas, 1939.**

Above right **Denim-clad cowboys gather around a branding fire, Custer National Forest, Montana, 1939.**

For many, there exist two denim jackets that are the benchmark for all others: the classic Levi's Trucker and the Lee Storm Rider. Of the two, the Levi's jacket has the longer history and has been through more changes than its Lee counterpart.

Beginning life in 1905, the Levi's denim blouse (as it was then known) was made from 9 oz denim and featured a single front pocket on the left, vertical pleats and a back cinch belt. Around 1953 the Type 2 jacket was developed, this time with two front pockets, bar tacks (reinforced stitching) to the seams and waist adjusters instead of the cinch.

The early 1960s saw the introduction of the Type 3 Trucker jacket – the one with which we are all probably most familiar. The shape was slimmed down and made slightly longer and the chest pockets given pointed flaps. This design has evolved slightly over the years, with the addition of side pockets, but remains fairly faithful to the 1960s original. The Type 1 and 2 jackets have also since been reproduced on the back of renewed interest in Levi's vintage heritage.

Lee produced its Storm Rider jacket in 1933 as a winter version of the Lee Rider jacket (also known as the 101) of 1931. With its shorter, sexier cut and distinctive Alaskan blanket lining and corduroy collar, it was an instant hit and became the denim jacket of choice for numerous style icons, including Steve McQueen.

Lee has looked to the original striped blanket lining for the detailing of its vintage-inspired range, the Lee 101 line, where it features on shirts, belts and wallets, as well as inside the classic Storm Rider, where it first appeared.

Above and right
Levi's Type 3 Trucker jacket.

Below right
Lee Storm Rider jacket.

Below **Spec drawing of the Levi's Type 3 Trucker jacket by Aaron Tubb, University of Westminster, London.**

Above **Street-style shots.**

Opposite **Early Type 3 Levi's Trucker jacket** at The Vintage Showroom.

THE FLYING JACKET

Vintage leather flying jackets.

The flying jacket, or flight jacket, started life during the First World War, when pilots flew in open cockpits and there was a real need for warm clothing. Towards the end of the war, in 1917, the US Army set up the Aviation Clothing Board, which distributed heavy-duty leather jackets to pilots and flight crew.

In the United Kingdom, the first sheepskin flying jacket was designed and manufactured by Leslie Irvin, who set up a manufacturing company in 1926 that went on to become the main supplier of flight jackets for the Royal Air Force during the Second World War. This bomber-style jacket, with zipped front and sheepskin-faced collar and revers, exists in many variations, as demand was so great that several manufacturers were eventually called upon to produce them.

On the other side of the Atlantic, in early 1931, the US Army Air Corps introduced the A-2 flight jacket, a waist-length jacket with ribbed cuffs and hem, made of seal-brown horsehide with a silk or cotton lining, which became standard issue. This jacket served for twelve years, until further developments were made and it was superseded. The Navy version of the flying jacket, the G-1, became the flight jacket of choice until 1978, when Congress decommissioned it because its popularity was overwhelming the supply system.

The emergence of the jet engine and the resulting new aircrafts meant the end of the leather flight jacket in active service, and it was replaced with lighter-weight synthetic jackets. However, the A-2 flight jacket was reissued in 1988 and it remains the benchmark for leather flying jacket design to this day.

Below **Vintage leather flying jacket.**

Opposite, clockwise from top left **'Headwear for Aviators'** vintage advertisement; an American pursuit pilot in combat gear set to climb into his plane; **'Clothing for Aviators'** vintage advertisement; Egil Johansen, who flew a Catalina aeroplane with supplies for the Norwegian resistance during the Second World War; Gieves flying helmet, worn for the Schneider Trophy seaplane race, *c.* 1925.

GARMENT BIOGRAPHIES 191

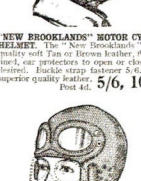

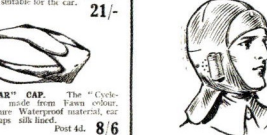

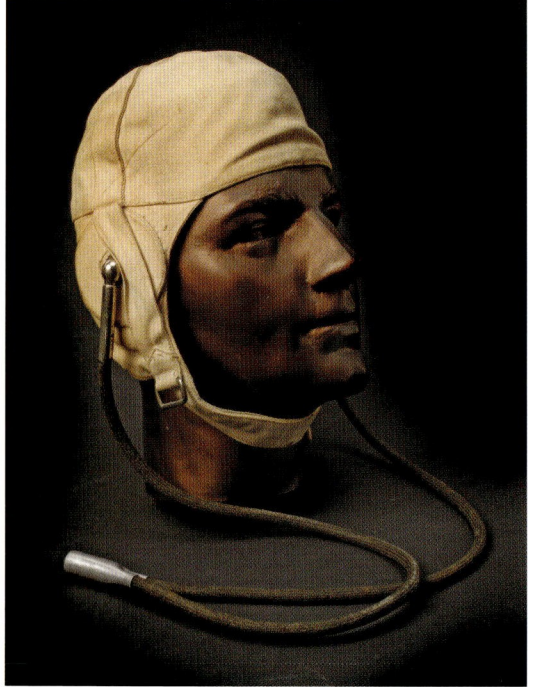

Left and above **Vintage flying jacket.**

Right **Lieutenant General George S. Patton in flying jacket, 30 March 1943.**

Below **Ladd Field, Alaska: Both Russians and Americans liked the brown-trimmed white 'Gaffney jacket' designed by Brigadier General Dale Gaffney,** c. 1943.

Opposite **Burberry sheepskin flight jacket, Autumn/Winter 2010.**

THE DUFFLE COAT

The duffle coat gains its name from the town of Duffel in Belgium's Antwerp province, where the locals traditionally made garments from the heavy, waterproof woollen 'duffel' cloth they produced.

First World War photographs show seamen in duffle-type coats with their distinctive wooden toggle and rope fastenings, capacious hood and trademark double yoke. In the interwar period the coat design grew into the now traditional naval duffle coat we know today. During the Second World War the coats were often known as convoy coats, and their popularity with Field Marshal Montgomery, who famously wore a camel-coloured duffle coat, also led to them being known as Monty coats.

In 1951 Gloverall was formed by Howard and Freda Morris, who had previously supplied the British Armed Forces with gloves and overalls and who had now been asked by the Ministry of Defence to dispose of its stock of Second World War and Korean War duffle coats. The supply of these coats eventually dwindled, but the demand was still very much there, so Gloverall began to manufacture duffle coats in a factory in London; the rope loop was replaced by a leather thong, a buffalo horn toggle was sourced, and the now-familiar double-faced checked cloth was introduced.

The company started exporting in the mid-1950s and it was not long before the coat achieved cult status. The sturdy, dependable duffle coat became the garment of choice for American beatniks and British 'Angry Young Men' – this was as much a political statement as an overcoat. In the United States, Perry Como and Bing Crosby were seen wearing theirs, and many celebrities, actors and sportsmen were pictured sporting a duffle coat – as was, of course, Paddington Bear.

Like other iconic pieces of clothing, the duffle coat has made the transition from utilitarian military garment to fashion staple. Versions appear regularly on the world's catwalks, and Gloverall continues to produce its classic more than sixty years after production began.

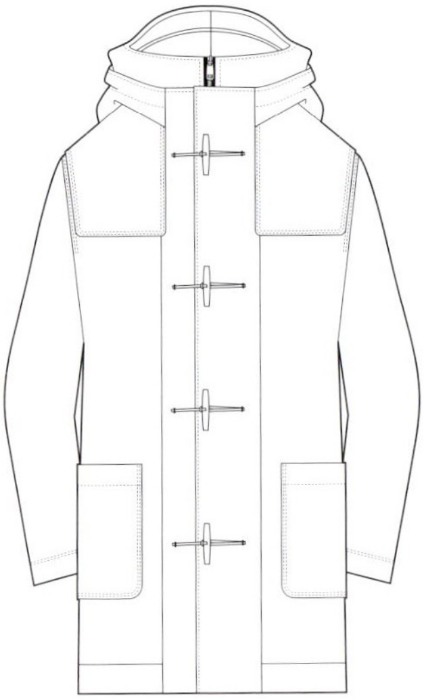

GARMENT BIOGRAPHIES 195

Opposite **Seamen in duffle coats.**

Clockwise from above **Spec drawings of a duffle coat by Aaron Tubb, University of Westminster, London; duffle coat being worn by a civilian, London, 1950s; teenager wearing a duffle coat, 1956; one of the first civilian duffles manufactured by Gloverall in the early 1950s and made from Loden wool fabric with rope and wooden toggles.**

Opposite **Paul Smith** duffle coat, Autumn/Winter 2011.

Above **Junya Watanabe** duffle-coat-inspired lightweight coat, Spring/Summer 2011.

Right Street-style shots.

198

GARMENT BIOGRAPHIES 199

Opposite **Gloverall** modern duffle coat.

Right **Gloverall's** re-creation of the original iconic duffle as worn throughout the Second World War by the Royal Navy and made famous by Field Marshal Montgomery.

THE FIELD JACKET

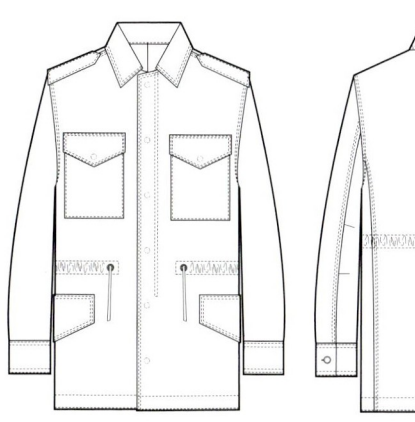

This page M-43 field jacket; spec drawings of a field jacket by Aaron Tubb, University of Westminster, London.

Opposite Robert De Niro as Travis Bickle wearing a field jacket in the film *Taxi Driver* (1976).

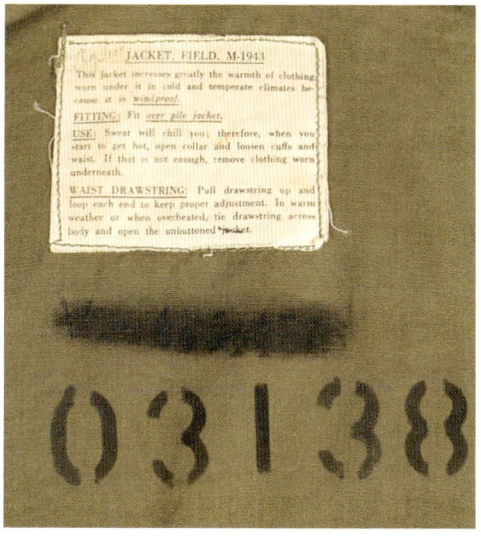

Above **Private E. G. Richards of Sterling, Illinois, wearing a field jacket while serving overseas as a truck driver in the United States Army.**

Opposite **Stone Island field jacket in Mussola Gommata, an exclusive fabric achieved by bonding an extremely light cotton muslin to a polyurethane film.**

When most people think field jacket, the M-65 is usually the first that comes to mind, but the the roots of this jacket itself go back to the Second World War M-43 (or M-1943) field jacket, a design so successful that military forces around the world still wear field jackets remarkably similar to it.

Based on the layering principle, the M-43 consisted of an olive-drab-cotton outer shell with layers added inside for additional warmth. There was a pile jacket liner for extremely cold areas, while the short wool jacket (the 'Ike' jacket) was worn in milder temperatures. An olive-drab-cotton cap was the head cover, and a fur-edged hood could also be added as an accessory.

Modified versions included the M-50 field jacket, with a button-in liner instead of a separate liner garment, and the M-51, which had a zip instead of buttons and metal snap closures for the pockets. This model remained in service until replaced by the famous M-65 – worn by the likes of Al Pacino in *Serpico* (1973) and Robert De Niro in *Taxi Driver* (1976). The M-65 was manufactured by Alpha Industries, in consultation with the US Army, and was originally made in olive green; it is now available in many different colours, as well as in camouflage prints. The jacket has two large lower pockets and two smaller chest pockets; a lightweight hood rolls out of the zipped collar; and, as with its predecessors, a thermal lining can be added. The M-65 now serves as inspiration for many of today's menswear brands. Stone Island, Abercrombie & Fitch and Belstaff, as well as innumerable others, all produce their homages to this practical and iconic jacket.

BIBLIOGRAPHY

Behrens, Roy R., *False Colors: Art, Design and Modern Camouflage*, Dysart, Iowa, 2002

Beirendonck, Walter Van, *Dream the World Awake*, Tielt, Belgium, 2012

Blechman, Hardy and Alex Newman, *DPM: Disruptive Pattern Material*, London, 2004

Bonami, Francesco, Maria Luisa Frisa and Stefano Tonchi, *Uniform: Order and Disorder*, Milan, 2001

Davies, Hywel, *Modern Menswear*, London, 2008

Facchinato, Daniela, *Ideas from Massimo Osti*, Bologna, 2012

Grand, France, *Comme des Garçons*, London, 1998

Griffiths, Nick and Francesco Morace, *Stone Island: Archives '982–'012*, Milan, 2012

Howell, Geraldine, *Wartime Fashion: From Haute Couture to Homemade, 1939–1945*, London, 2012

Huvenne, Paul, Emmanuelle Dirix and Bruno Blonde, *Black: Masters of Black in Fashion and Costume*, Antwerp, 2010

Jones, Terry, *Rei Kawakubo*, Cologne and London, 2012

Jones, Terry, *Yohji Yamamoto*, Cologne and London, 2012

Newark, Tim, *Camouflage*, London and New York, 2009

Sherwood, James, *Savile Row: The Master Tailors of British Bespoke*, London and New York, 2010

Sherwood, James, *The Perfect Gentleman: The Pursuit of Timeless Elegance and Style in London*, London and New York, 2012

Simms, Josh, Douglas Gunn and Roy Luckett, *Vintage Menswear: A Collection from The Vintage Showroom*, London, 2012

Sudjic, Deyan, *Rei Kawakubo and Comme des Garçons*, London, 1990

Thornton, Phil, *Casuals: Football, Fighting and Fashion – The Story of a Terrace Cult*, Lytham, 2013

www.style.com

ACKNOWLEDGMENTS

Kim Jones, Dylan Jones, Peter Tilley, Ike Rust, Christopher New, Andrew Groves, Stephanie Cooper, Richard Gray, Elinor Renfrew, Sean Chiles, Sharon Graubard, Nigel Cabourn, Drew Holmes, Aitor Throup, Mariel Reed, Frederick Dhyr, Amy Leverton, Walter Van Beirendonck, David Flamee, Anne Marie NG, Damien Arness-Dalton, Jonathan Quayle, Paul Frecker, Terry Jones, Doug Gunn, Alex Lee, Francesca Picciocchi, Sylvia Quayle, Chris Brooke, Barnzley, Richard De Pesando, Christopher Shannon, Federica De Carlo, Willem Kampert, Sarah Driscoll, Joseph O'Brien, Charlotte Sutcliffe-Smith, Blanaid Kenny, Holly Daws, Joe Knight, Cozette McCreery, Victor Hensel-Coe, David Scott Noble, Dr and Mrs Kirke, Simon Foxton, Emma Shackleton.

The staff and students at: Central Saint Martins, London; Kingston University, London; Royal College of Art, London; University of Westminster, London; AMFI, Amsterdam.

Louis Vuitton, MoMu Antwerp, Nigel Cabourn, Alexander McQueen, Gloverall, Baracuta, the Gieves & Hawkes Archive, Barbour, Basso & Brooke, Carhartt WIP, The Vintage Showroom, Walter Van Beirendonck, Aitor Throup, Black Style, Sibling, Stylesight, Timothy Everest, Stone Island, Rokit, Beyond Retro, Catwalking.com.

Detail of a Coldstream Guards bandsman's tunic and drum by Hawkes, early twentieth century.

ILLUSTRATION CREDITS

A: above; B: below; C: centre; L: left; R: right; T: top

1 Image by and courtesy of Basso & Brooke
2 Image by Pedrita Junckes, courtesy Basso & Brooke
7 Library of Nineteenth Century Photography
9 All images Library of Nineteenth Century Photography
10 Library of Congress Prints and Photographs Division, Washington D.C. (LC-USZC4-8766)
11 Hulton-Deutsch Collection/Corbis
12A Reg Speller/Fox Photos/Getty Images
12B Popperfoto/Getty Images
13 Collection Anne Finch
17 Victor Boyko/Getty Images
18 Collection of author
19 Images by Victor Hensel-Coe, thanks to Blackstyle, London N8
20 Francois Guillot/AFP/Getty Images
21 Catwalking
22 Catwalking
23 Alexander Klein/AFP/Getty Images
25 Victor Boyko/Getty Images
26 Thomas Giddings, courtesy Sibling
27 All images Thomas Giddings
28 Catwalking
29 AL: Library of Congress Prints and Photographs Division, Washington D.C. (LC-DIG-nclc-03576)
R: Library of Congress Prints and Photographs Division, Washington D.C. (LC-DIG-nclc-03583)
B: Library of Congress Prints and Photographs Division, Washington D.C. (LC-DIG-nclc-03850)
30–31 Courtesy Stylesight
31 Catwalking
32–33 All images Alex Telfer
36 Peter Willi/Superstock/Getty Images
37 Courtesy Alexander McQueen
38 Image by Victor Hensel-Coe
39 Images by Victor Hensel-Coe
40 Courtesy Christopher Shannon
41 Video still courtesy Christopher Shannon
44 Library of Nineteenth-Century Photography
46 Collection of author
47AL and CR: Courtesy Rokit
47AR: Courtesy Beyond Retro
48 Courtesy Gieves & Hawkes Archive, No. 1 Savile Row
49 Salomon Mesdach courtesy MoMu, Antwerp
50 Courtesy Stylesight
51 Courtesy Stylesight
53 Top row: Alex Lee
Middle: L Alex Lee, others courtesy Stylesight
Bottom: L Alex Lee, others courtesy Stylesight
54 John Dominis/Time Life Pictures/Getty Images
55 Garment shots courtesy Baracuta Hulton-Deutsch Collection/Corbis
56 Terry O'Neill/Getty Images
57 L: Catwalking / R: Catwalking
58 Library of Congress Prints and Photographs Division, Washington D.C. (LC-DIG-ggbain-16880)
59 Popperfoto/Getty Images
60 AR: Library of Congress Prints and Photographs Division, Washington D.C. (LC-DIG-ggbain-29394)
Others: Courtesy Jonathan Quayle collection
61 John Swope/Time Life Pictures/Getty Images
62 John Kobal Foundation/Getty Images
63 Francois Guillot/AFP/Getty Images
64 Image by Victor Hensel-Coe with thanks to The Vintage Showroom
65 L: John Chillingworth/Picture Post/Getty Images
R: Library of Nineteenth-Century Photography
66 Image courtesy Barbour
67 Image courtesy Barbour
68 All images courtesy Aitor Throup
69 All images courtesy Aitor Throup
70 Collection of author
71 L: Image by Victor Hensel-Coe
R: Catwalking
72 L: Catwalking
R: Courtesy Dr & Mrs Kirke
73 L: Gordon Wiltsie/National Geographic/Getty Images
R: Catwalking
76 L: Courtesy A Child of the Jago
R: Jane Sweeney/Lonely Planet Images/Getty Images
77 Courtesy Walter Van Beirendonck
79 Formal wear guide courtesy Sean Chiles Illustrations collection of author
84 Collection of author
85 L: Catwalking
AR: Collection of author
B: Image by Victor Hensel-Coe, with thanks to The Vintage Showroom
86 Courtesy of the Gieves & Hawkes Archive, No. 1 Savile Row
87 Courtesy of Gieves and Hawkes
88 Courtesy of Timothy Everest/Fashion and Textile Museum, London
89 Courtesy of Timothy Everest/Fashion and Textile Museum, London
90 A: Andrew MacPherson
B: Ruth Costello
91 Ruth Costello
92 Library of Congress/Science Faction/Getty Images
93 Collection of author
94 Francois Guillot/AFP/Getty Images
95 A: Library of Congress Prints and Photographs Division, Washington D.C. (LC-DIG-fsa-8a03304)
C: Library of Congress Prints and Photographs Division, Washington D.C. (LC-DIG-matpc-18058)
B: Library of Congress Prints and Photographs Division, Washington D.C. (LC-USF33-020849-M5)
96 A: Library of Nineteenth-Century Photography
B: Courtesy Dr & Mrs Kirke
97 A: Image courtesy the Gieves & Hawkes Archive, No. 1 Savile Row
L: Image by the author
R: Catwalking
100 Martino Lombezzi, courtesy Stone Island
101 Photography: Nick Griffiths. Styling: Simon Foxton
102–103 Martino Lombezzi, courtesy Stone Island
104 Courtesy Beyond Retro
105 A: Image courtesy Carhartt WIP
B: Courtesy Beyond Retro
106 L: Image courtesy Stone Island, from the book Stone Island, Archivio '982–'012 Photography: Nick Griffiths. Styling: Simon Foxton
R: Catwalking
108 Courtesy A Child of the Jago
109 B: Image courtesy the Gieves & Hawkes Archive, No. 1, Savile Row
110 L: Collection of author
R: Library of Nineteenth-Century Photography
111 L: Library of Nineteenth-Century Photography
R: Collection of Damien Arness-Dalton
112 AC: Library of Congress Prints and Photographs Division, Washington D.C. (LC-USZC4-1292)
R: Catwalking
B: Collection of author
113 CR: Library of Congress Prints and Photographs Division, Washington D.C. (LC-USF33-T01-000375-M1)
BL: Catwalking
BR: Library of Congress Prints and Photographs Division, Washington D.C. (LC-USF33-011919-M4)
114 L: Courtesy Rokit
R: Victor Hensel-Coe with thanks to The Vintage Showroom
115 CL: Library of Congress Prints and Photographs Division, Washington D.C. (LC-DIG-fsa-8a03304)
116 L: Courtesy Rokit
R: Courtesy Guido Kerssens, AMFI, Amsterdam
117 L: Library of Congress Prints and Photographs Division, Washington, D.C., 20540 USA
R: Fotosearch/Getty Images
118 A: Courtesy Beyond Retro
B: By the author
119 Collection of author; Victor Hensel-Coe
120 L: Courtesy Carhartt WIP
R: Collection of author
121 Collection of author; David Scott Noble
122 L: Courtesy Dickies
B: Courtesy Shelley Fox, Parsons New School, New York
123 Courtesy Dickies
124 Ruth Costello, courtesy Timothy Everest
125 Alex Telfer, courtesy Nigel Cabourn Loom: courtesy of Guido Kerssens, AMFI, Amsterdam
126 L: George Silk/Time Life Pictures/Getty Images

127 L: Catwalking
R: Catwalking
128 Victor Hensel-Coe, with thanks to The Vintage Showroom
129 Clockwise: Jean-Erick Pasquier/ Gamma-Rapho/Getty Images
Catwalking Collection of author
130 all: Collection of author
131 Thomas Giddings, courtesy Sibling
132 Image by Dan Lecca, courtesy Walter Van Beirendonck
133 Images by Alex Telfer, photography courtesy Nigel Cabourn
136 L: Library of Nineteenth Century Photography
R: Collection of author
137 A: Collection of author
B: Collection of author
138 Courtesy Rokit
139 Clockwise: Courtesy Beyond Retro
Library of Congress Prints and Photographs Division, Washington D.C. (LC-USZ62-133650)
Courtesy Beyond Retro
Courtesy Matt Williams
Courtesy Matt Williams
140 Dan Lecca, courtesy Walter Van Beirendonck
142 Pierre Verdy/AFP/Getty Images
143 Pierre Verdy/AFP/Getty Images
144–45 All images courtesy Aitor Throup
148 Jordan Jennings, courtesy XXBC
149 Alex Lee
154 Catwalking
157 Portrait: Roland Stoops
Others: Dan Lecca
160 Kirn Vintage Stock/Corbis
161 Clockwise: Collection of author
Image courtesy Oldmagazinearticles.com
Image courtesy Oldmagazinearticles.com
Garment images courtesy Rokit
162 Giuseppe Cacace/AFP/Getty Images
163 Courtesy A Child of the Jago
164 Clockwise: Collection of author
Heritage Images/Corbis
Oldmagazinearticles.com
165 Sally Cook
166 A: Courtesy Rokit
B: Sally Cook
167 AL: Sally Cook
AR and B: Victor Hensel-Coe
168 Courtesy Charles Kirke
169 Catwalking
171 Courtesy Central Saint Martins, London
173 Clockwise: Catwalking
Library of Congress Prints and Photographs Division, Washington D.C. (LC-DIG-fsa-8a03304)
Library of Congress Prints and Photographs Division, Washington D.C. (LC-USF33-020849-M5)
174 Keystone/Getty Images
175 Courtesy Rokit
176–77 Images by Victor Hensel-Coe, with thanks to Blackstyle, London N8
178 L: Catwalking
R: Courtesy Beyond Retro
179 David Scott Noble
180 Keystone/Hulton Archive/Getty Images
181 John Springer Collection/Corbis
182 Courtesy Beyond Retro
183 Catwalking
184 AL: Library of Congress Prints and Photographs Division, Washington D.C. (LC-USF33-012294-M2)
AR: Library of Congress Prints and Photographs Division, Washington D.C. (LC-USZ62-133650)
185 Clockwise: Courtesy Beyond Retro
Courtesy Rokit
186 Courtesy Stylesight
187 Image by Victor Hensel-Coe, with thanks to The Vintage Showroom
188 Courtesy Beyond Retro
189 Courtesy Beyond Retro
190 Courtesy Beyond Retro
191 Clockwise: Collection of author
Library of Congress Prints and Photographs Division, Washington D.C. (LC-DIG-fsa-8a05969)
Collection of author
Image courtesy Einar Garnes/ Gerd Garnes
Image courtesy the Gieves & Hawkes Archive, No. 1 Savile Row
192 AL and details: Courtesy Rokit
CR: Library of Congress Prints and Photographs Division, Washington D.C. (LC-USZ62-25122)
BC: Library of Congress Prints and Photographs Division, Washington D.C. (LC-USW33-053754-ZC)
193 Catwalking
194 Courtesy Gloverall
195 Daily Herald Archive/SSPL/Getty Images
Image courtesy Gloverall
196 Catwalking
197 A: Catwalking
197 B: Courtesy Stylesight.
198 Courtesy Gloverall
199 Courtesy Gloverall
200 Courtesy Rokit
201 Michael Ochs Archive/Getty Images
202 Library of Congress Prints and Photographs Division, Washington D.C. (LC-USW3-028129-E)
203 Styling by Simon Foxton, photo by Nick Griffiths courtesy Stone Island
204 Courtesy the Gieves & Hawkes Archive, No. 1, Savile Row
207 Library of Nineteenth-Century Photography
208 Library of Nineteenth-Century Photography

INDEX

Page numbers in *italic* refer to illustrations

Abercrombie & Fitch 16, 65, 202
Ackerman, Haider 155
Adidas 136
Africa 72, 73, *74*, *96*, 155
Albert, Prince 86
Alexandrou, Marios 150–51
Alfonso of Spain, King 78
Alpha 172, 202
Anderson & Sheppard 80
Anderson, J. W. 141
Angel's, Berman's and Nathan's 36
Antwerp Six 156
Apple Corps 88

Armitage, Simon 'Barnzley' 44–45
Austin Reed 89
Avirex 172

Bailey, Christopher 18
Bain, Sally 18
Balmain *169*
Baracuta 55, *55*
Barbour 16, 65, 66–67
baseball jackets 138–39
Bates, Joe 26–27
Beatles, The 88–89
Beau, Christine 150
Belovitch 70
Belstaff 38, 70–71, 202
Beuys, Joseph 36

Beyond Retro 47
Biddle, Anthony Drexel 78
Bikkembergs, Dirk 156
Blackaller, Connie 108
Blahnik, Manolo 89
Blanks, Tim 21, 22, 36
blazers 84–85
Boateng, Oswald 81
Bogart, Humphrey 160
'Bold Look' 9
Bowie, David *56*
Brandelli, Carlo 80
Brando, Marlon 11, 119, 178, *181*
Brooks Brothers 21
Broome, Will *26*, 130
Brown, Peter 88
Browne, Thom 15, 20–21, 129, 141

Bruce, Maggie 130
Brunt, Laurens 82–83
Bryan, Sid 26–27
Burberry 16, 18, *18–19*, 65, 70, 93, 160, *162*, 193
Burton 10
Burton, Sarah 36
Butcher of Blue 124
Byrne, Jack *80*

C. P. Company 68–69, 100, 144
Cabourn, Nigel 7, 32–35, 49, *125*, *133*
Caine, Michael 80
Calki, Yasemin *81*
camouflage *96*, 104–107

INDEX

Carhartt 65, *105*, 110, 120–21, 126, 142
cartes de visite 9
Central Saint Martins, London 6, 15, 17, 36, 40, 74–75, *134–35*, 141, *170–71*
Chanel, House of 66
Chapman, Jake and Dinos 24
Charles, Prince of Wales 80
Charlotte, Queen 86
Chen Jiagang 150
Child of the Jago, A *74*, *163*
Colley, Richard 44–45, *65*
Comme des Garçons 22–23, 28, 43, 142
Como, Perry 194
Converse 142
Cooper, Martin 70
Cooper, Stephanie 15, 141
Corre, Joseph 43, 45
Coward, Noël 80
Cox, Stephen 141
Crandall, James Otis 'Doc' *139*
Cromwell, Oliver 108
Crosby, Bing 194
Cubism 104
Cunningham, Bill 52

DAKS 46, 90
Davidson, Carolyn 136
Dawson Denim 124
De Niro, Robert *201*, 202
Dean, James 11, 56, 119, 178
Demeulemeester, Ann 156
'demob' suits 9–10
Denham 124
denim 38, *112–13*, 114–15, *116*, 119, 120, 124–25, 126, 142; jackets 182–87
Dickies *122*, *123*, *123*
Dietrich, Marlene 80
Dior 56, *57*, *127*
Dolce & Gabbana *113*
Doma, Damir 72
Donaldson, Williamson & Ward 88
Duckie Brown 141
Dudley, Earls of *86*
duffle coats 194–99
Duke, John 28
Dunhill 24

Edward VII 80, 130
Edward VIII *see* Windsor, Duke of
Elizabeth II 86
Elliott, Tascha *109*
Engineered Garments 111
Esquire 9
Everest, Timothy 7, 89, 90–91, *124*

Fair Isle *26*, 130–35
Ferrari, Moreno 68
field jackets 200–203
Finch, Anne *11*
Flat Head 124
Flügel, John Carl 8
flying jackets 188–93
Ford, Tom 89
formal wear 78–79, 98
Fox Brothers & Co. *91*

Frankel, Susannah 70
Fred Perry 55

Gaffney, Brigadier General Dale *192*
Gallagher, Liam 172
Galliano, John 43, *63*, 72, *73*, 89
Galt, James 86
Gandiaga, Goioiza Ferreras *78*
Gaultier, Jean Paul 50, *97*
George III 86
George IV 58
George V 86
Gieves 80, 86–87, *191*
Gieves & Hawkes *97*, *109*
Gloverall 194, *195*, *198*, *199*
GQ 79, 81
Grant, Cary 56, 80
Grant, Patrick 81
Graubard, Sharon 15, 16, 45, 50, 52, 62, 141
Gray, Richard 17, 49
Greenwood, Charlotte *62*
Grosberg, Harry 70
Groves, Andrew 15–16, 63, 141
G-Star 124
Guardian, The 18
Gucci 114
Guevara, Ernesto 'Che' 70
Gunn, Douglas 38
Gushue, Thomas *173*

Hackett 16, 65
Harlech, Amanda 66
Harley-Davidson 178
Harper's Bazaar 10
Harrington jackets 54–55
Harris 58
Hillary, Edmund 32
Himalayas *17*, 24, 72
Hinde, J. F. K. *65*
Hindmarch, Anya 66
Hint 155
Hitchcock, Alfred 80
Hodges, Liam 146–47
Howey, Thomas 72

i-D 52
Iron Heart 124
Irvin, Leslie 190

Jack Knife 124
Jack Wills 16, 65
Jacobs, Marc 43
Jagger, Mick and Bianca 89
James, Richard 81
Jantzen 136
J. C. Penney 10
Jil Sander 43
Johansen, Egil *191*
John, Elton 89
Jones, Dylan 79, 81
Jones, Ken 24
Jones, Kim 7, 65, 72, 150
Jones, Stephen 24
Jones, Terry 52

Kasabian 144
Kawakubo, Rei 22, 28, 45, 142, 144
Keaton, Buster *62*, 63
Kilgour, French & Stanbury 80
King, Clandon Layton 111
Kingston University, London 150–51
Kirke, Charles 93, *168*
Klein, Calvin 43, 114
KOI 124
Kusama, Yayoi 150
Kwok, Kelvin 76–77

Labelux Group 70
Lacoste 136
Lagerfeld, Karl 66
Langlitz Leathers 178, *180*
Lanvin 56, *57*
Larocca, Amy 21
Lauren, Ralph 16, 21, 30–31, 65
L. C. King Manufacturing Company 111

Lee 52, *53*, 118–19, 148, *148*, 184, *185*
letterman's jackets 138–39
Leverton, Amy 124
Levi Strauss 114, 116–17, 126, 142, *182*, 184, *185*, *186*
Lewis Leathers 178
Livingstone, David 80
Lloyd, Henri 16
Loew, William Goadby 78
Loewe 142
London 10, *11*, 18, *21*, 26, 36, 38, 43, 45, 49, 50, 52, 56, 80, 81, 88, 89, 90, 144, 194, *195*
Lou, Philip *115*
Luckiett, Roy 38
Lyle & Scott 142

MA.STRUM 16
Margiela 126, 151
Marks & Spencer 90
Martens, Dr. 55
McCreery, Cozette 26–27, 130

Right and overleaf
Victorian gentlemen

McDonald's 155
McGrady, Alexander 113
McLaren, Malcolm 43, 45
McQueen, Alexander 36–37, 43, 45
McQueen, Steve 54, 55, 56, 66
Meredith, Melchisedek 86
Mesdach, Salomon 49
Meyer, Louis B. 80
military wear 16, 38, 45
modernism 22
Moncler 21
Montgomery, Field Marshal 194, 198
Morris, Howard and Frida 194
Morrison, Arthur 45
motorcycle jackets 178–81

Neilson, Rebecca 47
Nelson, Admiral Lord 86
'New Edwardian Look' 10
New York 15, 21, 45, 49, 50, 52, 58, 111, 141, 148
New York magazine 21
New York Times, The 28, 52
NEWGEN MEN 40
Nicoll, Richard 43
Nike 136
Niven, David 80
Norton & Son 81
Nutter, Tommy 79, 80–81, 88–89, 90

O'Neal, Ryan 55
Ohfuchi, Takeshi 111
oilskins 128–29
Osborne, Captain George B. 126
Osti, Massimo 68, 100

Pacino, Al 202
Paddington Bear 194
Pak, Christopher 93, 173
Paris 20, 21, 28, 52, 63, 72, 81, 155
parkas 172–77
Parsons The New School, New York 122
Patton, Lieutenant General George 192
Pawson, James 152–53
pea coats 164–69
Peal & Co. 58
Peary, Robert 173
Penrose, Roland 104
Peru 74
Pet Shop Boys 172
Peters, Amelia 134–35
Philip, Prince 86
Phoenix Lettering 138
Pitti Immagine Uomo 81
Pizzorno, Sergio 144
Pointer 111
Poole, Henry 80
Post Overalls 111
Prada 43
Presley, Elvis 55
Prince Regent 8
Puma 142
Pungetti, Alessandro 68

Rag & Bone 112–13
Railcar Fine Goods 124

Raleigh 124
Richards, Private E. G. 202
Rodic, Yvan 52
Rokit 47, 192
Rolling Stones, The 89
Royal College of Art, London 15, 17, 68, 144, 146–47
RRL 30–31
Rust, Ike 15, 16

Sander, August 28, 45
Savile Row 7, 10, 36, 45, 56, 58, 80–81, 86, 88–89, 90, 126, 141
Scholte 58
Schott 178, 179
Schuffenecker, Claude-Emile 36
Scotch & Soda 124
Scott, Charlotte 126
Sears 10
Sedgwick, Edward 62
Sexton, Edward 88–89
Shannon, Christopher 40–41
Sherwood, James 81
Shipp, Reginald 9
Sibling 26–27, 130, 131
Silver, Daniel 141
Simons, Raf 43, 93, 151, 155
Simpson, Wallis 58, 60, 60
Sims, David 36
Sinatra, Frank 56, 80
6876 15
Smith, Paul 49, 65, 66, 82, 196
Solomon, Solomon J. 104
sportswear 38, 45, 64, 98, 136–37, 141
Stanley, H. M. 80
Steele, Richard 108
Stone Island 49, 68, 93, 100–101, 106, 144, 202, 203
Strawbridge, Philip 170–71
street style 52–53
Style.com 21, 22, 36, 72
Stylesight 15, 16, 45, 50, 50, 52, 53, 62, 124, 141, 197
Sugar Cane 124
Suzuki, David 111

Tailor & Cutter 79
Tchernawitz, Jack 173
Ten C 16
Thompson, Will 148, 148
Throup, Aitor 68–69, 141, 144–45
Tokyo 22, 28, 142
trench coats 160–63
Trickers 142
Tubb, Aaron 98–99, 107, 122, 123, 161, 166, 172, 185, 195, 200

uniforms 32, 45, 92–97, 98, 104, 108–109, 141
Utility scheme 9, 11

Valentino, Rudolph 80
Van Beirendonck, Walter 62, 75, 132, 140–41, 141, 155, 156–57
Vanderbilt, Gloria 114
Van Noten, Dries 73, 85, 106, 156
Van Saene, Dirk 156
Vanson 142, 178
Victoria, Queen 86

Viktor & Rolf 15, 155
Vintage Showroom, The 38–39, 64, 71, 85, 114, 129, 187
Vuitton, Louis 7, 16, 17, 24–25, 65, 72

W magazine 70
Wang, Yangzi 91
Watanabe, Junya 22, 43, 94–95, 111, 127, 141, 142–43, 173, 178, 197
Watson, Eric 172
Wayne/Jayne County 27
Weaver, Aiden 17
Wellington, Duke of 86
Wenders, Wim 28
Wendy & Jim 155
Westminster, University of, London 6, 7, 15, 17, 17, 18, 47, 63, 78, 80, 81, 93, 98–99, 107, 108, 109, 113, 115, 126, 141, 152–53, 161, 172, 173, 185, 195, 200

westminsterfashion 18
Westwood, Vivienne 43, 45, 89, 155
Willhelm, Bernhard 49, 141, 154–55
Windsor, Duke of 8, 58–61, 78, 96
Women's Wear Daily 52
Wood, Charles 164
Work in Progress 120–21
workwear 16, 32, 38, 45, 110–13, 122–23, 142, 178

XXBC 141, 148–49

Yamamoto, Yohji 28–29, 45, 72
Yee, Marina 156

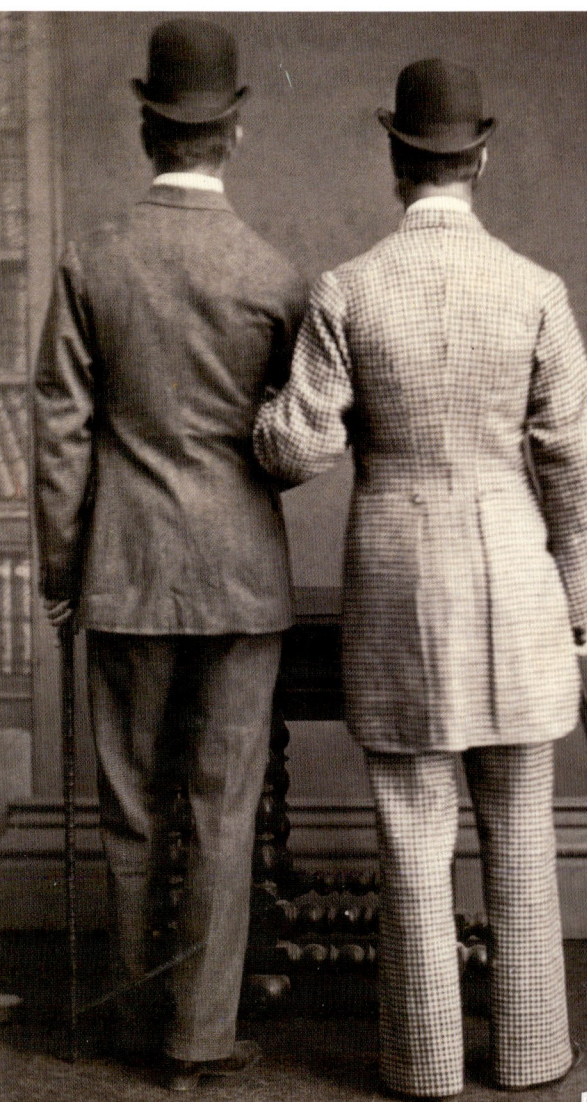